Coaching the Flip-Flop
Basketball Offense

Jimmy
Earle

Coaching the Flip-Flop Basketball Offense

Parker Publishing Company, Inc.
West Nyack, N.Y.

PRINTED IN THE UNITED STATES OF AMERICA

B.C. (13-139261-1)

"Try not the Pass!" the old man said; "Dark lowers the tempest overhead, the roaring torrent is deep and wide!" and loud that clarion voice replied, "Excelsior!"

Dedication

I would like to dedicate this book to my loving wife Frances and my little boy and girl, Jimmy Jr. and Tammye Lynn. To my wonderful parents Pat and Iva Earle. To the late Dr. Quill E. Cope, a friend of athletics.

Acknowledgments

I would like to acknowledge the following people who played an important part in the writing of this manuscript:

To Coach Joe Nunley, my fine high school coach, who introduced me to and taught me how to play the game of basketball.

To Coach Kermit Smith, my fine junior college basketball coach and athletic director at Martin Junior College, for his guidance and encouragement.

To Dr. W. C. Westenberger, President of Martin Junior College for his support and friendship during my four years at Martin College.

To Coach Charles Murphy, Middle Tennessee's great football coach and present athletic director, for his wonderful inspiration and friendship.

To Coach Ken "Trick" Trickey, for giving me the opportunity to assist him in the fine basketball program at Middle Tennessee State University.

To Coach John Oldham, Western Kentucky's great basketball coach, for writing the foreword for this book and for his encouragement to me during my coaching career.

To Angie Defronzo for his help in scouting.

Finally, I would like to pay tribute to the following: To my good friends Bob Brooks, Dr. Bob Womack, Dr. E. K. Patty, Dr. John Weems, Dr. Harry Wagner and Dr. Stanley Hall for their encouragement and support. Mr. Bill Pack and Coach Jack Deere for all their friendship and help during my coaching career. Coach Terry Sweeney for his friendship.

Ken Lannom and Gene Crippen, our student assistants at Middle Tennessee.

My good friend, Bill Burks, head of the Department of English at Martin College, for editing the manuscript. Mrs. Roxie McHenry, for typing part of the manuscript and to John Paul Montgomery for his proofreading. Mr. Herman Masin, editor of *Scholastic Coach,* for publishing my basketball articles. And also to the wonderful athletes I have coached in high school, junior college, and senior college.

Foreword

Whether you have been coaching for one year or 20 years you can certainly benefit from reading this book written by Coach Jimmy Earle. I have had the pleasure of following the progress of this energetic and promising young coach since his high school coaching days. All of his teams have been well versed in the basic rudiments of the game. Now, he exposes his Flip-Flop Offense which I have seen in successful operation.

Jim is a basketball nut. He lives, breathes, and sleeps the game. You will find as you are reading the book that his enthusiasm is infectious. It has been a pleasure for me to recommend this knowledgeable book of updated basketball material for your reading.

JOHN OLDHAM
Head Basketball Coach
Western Kentucky University

The How and Why
of the Flip-Flop Offense

The modern-day game of basketball features jet-powered fast breaks, rigged-up pressure defenses, and continuity and semi-continuity offenses. These trends have helped basketball develop into one of the greatest spectator sports of all time.

The offensive systems employed today must be flexible enough to adjust to the changing trends in the game of basketball, and, indeed, may be gauged by their ability to withstand the test of time. A prime criterion for a modern-day offense would be its ability to operate effectively against pressure defenses. The defenses of today do not sit back merely waiting to see what the offense is going to do; they move up on the 10-second line to apply pressure and to force offensive floor mistakes, bad passes, altered cutting routes, and so forth.

The Flip-Flop Offensive System thrives on the pressure defenses, meeting them head-on and exploiting their weaknesses.

Originated by Football Coach Darrel Royal of the University of Texas, Flip-Flop refers to the offense's ability to be run from either side of the field with the same personnel. The Flip-Flop Offense is designed to make possible the high percentage shot. Looking first for the lay-up and then for the short or medium range jump shot, this offense on many occasions will free an individual player for a wide-open, unmolested lay-up.

The Flip-Flop is unique among continuity offenses in that it offers the coach a chance to explore the special talents of certain players while still using a continuity offense (many other continuity offenses will rotate these players away from their strong area). For example, with the Flip-Flop the post men are interchangeable (high and low) but are never rotated outside where they lose their effectiveness on the boards.

One of the most important features of the Flip-Flop Offense is its ability to operate as effectively against zone defenses as against the man-to-man defense, with a minimum of pattern adjustment. When the opponent continues to harass by changing defenses on the floor and "matching up," the successful offense must be capable of countering these rigged-up defenses.

The Flip-Flop Offense has been highly successful for me on three different levels of basketball competition: high school, junior college, and senior college. The ability of this offense to adapt itself to the different levels of competition has been tremendous.

In presenting the Flip-Flop Offense, let me emphasize to you that it is by no means completely original. This offense is the culmination of many ideas which I picked up from coaching clinics, basketball articles, viewing game films, through articles, and through practical experimentation. For example, the basic floor positions of the Flip-Flop are the same as that of the Shuffle offense. The Shuffle, of course, is one of the most widely utilized basketball offenses of all time. It was originated by Bruce Drake, a pioneer in basketball coaching circles, and later developed by Joel Eaves at Auburn University. Although the floor positions of the Shuffle and the Flip-Flop are the same, the movements and rotations are completely different. The Flip-Flop patterns, featuring clear-outs, screen and rolls, weaves, etc., offer the individual players much more freedom than the other continuity offenses.

The Flip-Flop, like many other of the modern-day offenses, is initiated from a single-post alignment. The offense is similar to them also in the fact that it emphasizes movement, ball exchange, and screening both on and off of the ball. Its adaptability to a wide range of personnel offers a coach, regardless of the level of competition, excellent offensive patterns.

JIMMY EARLE

Contents

Symbols Used in Diagrams

1-2-3-4-5   *Offensive Players*

    X   *Defensive Players*

-----➤   *Pass*

〰➤   *Dribble*

———⊣   *Screen*

———↙   *Screen and Roll*

———➤   *Movement of Player*

···>   *Rebound*

Coaching the Flip-Flop
Basketball Offense

1

The Flip-Flop Versus
the Man-to-Man Defenses

The Flip-Flop Offense is initiated from a two-guard front. The basic setup of the offense is an overload on the side of the high-post man and the high forward. The offense is also a tandem post offense featuring a high and low post with the weak-side forward as the low-post man. Since the Flip-Flop is a continuity offense featuring interchanging floor positions, we shall not list the desired characteristics of each position, since they are interchangeable, and because all five players are rotated constantly once the offense is initiated. The floor positions are as shown in Diagram 1.

The *strong-side guard* (number 1) sets up halfway between forward 3 and high-post man 5. When initiating the offense he should penetrate this area as deep as the defense will allow him. This floor position allows the strong-side guard equal passing routes to the forward, the high post, and the weak-side guard. It allows the strong-side guard a much better cutting angle off the high-post man and is also a good cutting angle if he wants to go outside the forward.

The *weak-side guard* (number 2) sets head up on the basket; that is, he is directly in front of the basket and two steps directly behind the head of the free-throw lane. The weak-side guard will also penetrate as deep as the defense will allow him when initiating any pattern in the Flip-Flop. The weak-side guard's floor position on the weak side enables him to feed the strong-side guard (number 1), the weak-side low forward (number 4), and receive a pass from the strong-side guard and hit back to the weak side after an exaggerated overplay by the defense. The weak-side guard will not be able to feed the high-post man at the basic high-post position, but he will be able to feed the high-post man if he rolls across the lane high and moves to meet the ball.

The *strong-side forward* (number 3) sets up at a high forward position. His floor position is two steps inside the sidelines and directly even with the foul lane extended. In some instances, if the forward is having a hard time receiving a pass from the strong-side guard because the defensive forward is overplaying him, the strong-side forward may set up lower and move out to meet the pass. The strong-side forward's floor position will vary according to the defensive alignment and the quickness and overplay of the defensive forward. However, the high position is the most desirable in the execution of the offense, as the pass from the guard is easier to receive at this position. This position also opens up the lane and allows the high-post man more freedom to operate.

The *weak-side forward,* or the low forward (number 4), sets up at a low baseline post position. He lines up directly to the side of the lane as close to the lane as possible and one step up from the baseline. When receiving a pass from the weak-side guard (number 2), the weak-side forward moves out to receive the ball as close to the goal as the defensive man will allow him. He is also in the passing routes of the high-post man (number 5), and by breaking across the lane, the strong-side forward (number 3). The weak-side forward's floor position allows him to rebound the weak-side board exclusively and offers him many easy tip-in opportunities.

The *high-post man's* (number 5) basic floor position is a high-post set at the side of the foul lane extended and as close to the key as possible. The high-post man is actually the hub or the center of the offense, as he is involved in most of the screening situations either on or off the ball. The high-post man is also what is known as the "safety valve" in the offense. By this we mean that whenever the passing lanes in the offense are overplayed or clogged, the high-post man must work himself open to receive a pass. We tell our high-post man he must "hunt daylight" whenever our offense is

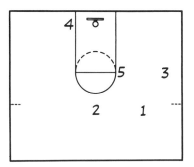
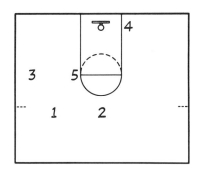

Diagram 1   *Diagram 2*

pressured. His primary rebounding responsibility is the middle of the lane in setting up the offensive rebounding triangle.

In Diagram 2 the Flip-Flop setup on the opposite side of the floor is illustrated with the same alignment as in Diagram 1.

In listing the offense and the floor positions, you will notice the strong side of the floor has the odd numbers (1 & 3), the weak side, the even (2 & 4). This system of numbering simplifies the learning process of position by numbers.

THE INITIATION OF THE FLIP-FLOP

The initiation of the Flip-Flop Offense is broken down into four phases: (1) guard-to-strong-side forward (inside and outside cut); (2) guard-to-guard; (3) guard-to-weak-side forward; and (4) guard-to-high post. The guard-to-high-post initiation in the Flip-Flop is utilized as a release against the pressure defenses. The guard-to-high-post initiation and the other releases utilized to combat modern pressure defenses will be discussed in detail in the second chapter.

GUARD-TO-STRONG-SIDE FORWARD INITIATION

Diagram 3 illustrates the first option of the guard-to-strong-side forward. G^1 passes to F^3 and cuts to either side of high-post 5 (in the early initiations he will be able to take the inside cuts). If G^1 takes the inside cut, the high-post man steps up a full step and offers a stationary pick for 1's cut to the basket as shown in Diagram 4.

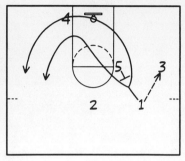 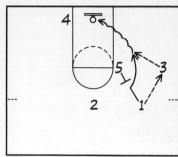

Diagram 3   *Diagram 4*

If G^1 can maneuver the defensive man into high-post 5's screen, then F^3 feeds him on his inside cut. However, in most cases high-post man 5's defensive man will sag and take the cutter down the lane. In this case, F^3 passes to high-post 5 as he rolls a couple of steps down the lane for a jump shot (Diagram 5).

In Diagram 6, G^1 passes to F^3 and is body-checked by the defensive man. G^1 then cuts away from F^3 and opens up the area for a two-on-two play by F^3 and high-post 5.

After the initiation pass to F^3 and G^1's cut, high-post 5 steps out and sets a pick on F^3's defensive man. F^3 comes over the top of the screen for a jump shot. If the defense switches, F^3 can feed high-post 5 on the roll to the basket. In the event 5 does not receive the ball, then he rolls across the lane and waits to see the offense develop before determining his next move (Diagram 7).

Diagram 8 shows the rotation of the players after the first option of the Flip-Flop is completed.

NOTE: G^1, who made the initial pass to F^3, has cut through and set up at the strong-side forward. Weak-side forward 4 sets up at the high post; weak-side guard 2 is the strong-side guard. F^3 has moved out to weak-side guard, and high-post 5 sets at the weak-side forward or low post.

The second-guard option in the guard-to-forward initiation series is shown in Diagram 9.

The second-guard option is available whenever F^3 comes over

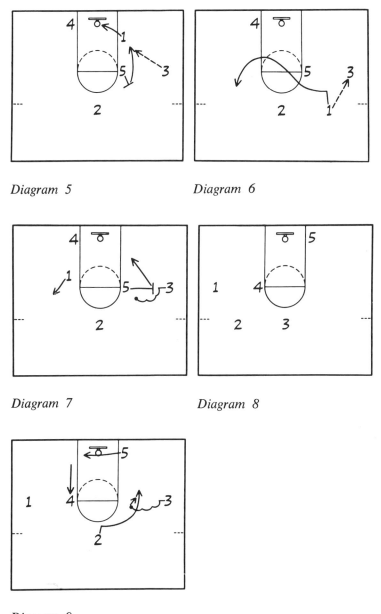

Diagram 5

Diagram 6

Diagram 7

Diagram 8

Diagram 9

the top of the high-post man's screen and he does not have a jump
shot or a good one-on-one situation, or when 5 is not open on the

roll. F^3 then, on the moving dribble, goes hard to the edge of the foul lane extended. Weak-side guard 2 times his move accordingly, and at the moment F^3 picks up his dribble at the edge of the key, weak-side guard 2 cuts off of F^3 and takes a hand-off for either a jump shot or a driving lay-up.

NOTE: This option has been found to be very effective in instances where the defensive high-post man guarding 5 switches on F^3 coming over the screen. In this situation the defensive man is too far on the inside of F^3 to react and take G^2 on his cut by F^3. The rotation on the second-guard option is shown in Diagram 10.

NOTE: 5 holds his position across the lane until the ball comes back out front; he then moves back across the lane.

G^1 sets up at forward on the opposite side of the floor; 4 moves up to the high post; 5 has rolled down and holds his position under the goal. F^3, after handing off, steps out either for a jump shot or to be ready to fill the strong-side guard position. G^2, if no shot is available, will come outside to the weak-side guard position. If G^2 takes a jump shot on the hand-off, the rebounding responsibilities are as follows: 5 rebounds his present position, 4 has middle responsibility, 2 will rebound his side after the shot, and 1 will take high lane rebound area.

Second-Guard Post Option

Diagrams 11A and 11B illustrate our second-guard post option if 2 finds himself unable to maneuver on the second-guard option.

After receiving the hand-off from 3 in the second-guard option, 2 finds himself covered. F^3 has stepped out either for a jump shot or a pass to start the offense from the other side of the floor. This move has opened the lane for 4, who is now the high-post man on the opposite side of the floor. 4 has the opportunity, when he sees 2 is covered, to either roll straight down the lane for a pass or roll across the lane and work a two-on-two (big man–little man situation) with 2. The lane option is diagramed in 11A, and the two-on-two situation with 4 and 2 is shown in Diagram 11B. The rotation is the same for both options.

In Diagram 12, we see the rotation for the second-guard post option. Post man 4, after his move down or across the lane, sets up at the low post. 5, who has stationed himself under the basket

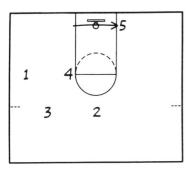

Diagram 10

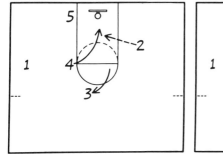

Diagram 11A

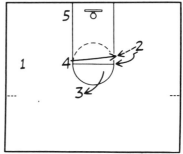

Diagram 11B

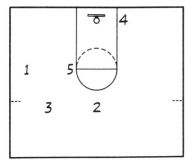

Diagram 12

after his roll under on the first option, fills 4's vacated high-post position. F³ has stepped out and filled the strong-side guard position.

2 has filled the weak-side guard position; 1 has set up at the strong-side forward.

You will note we have pulled F³, who was initially a forward, out on the floor and rotated the high- and low-post men 4 and 5.

GUARD-TO-CORNER OR GUARD-OUTSIDE OPTION

The guard-to-corner or guard-outside option is also initiated by a pass from a guard to a forward. The guard-to-corner option is a countermove against defenses that body-check the guards on their inside cutting routes. In order for the Flip-Flop to be effective, the guard must go outside against sagging or body-checking defenses that tend to bog down an offense or make it static. This option also tends to spread the defense out and opens up the head of the key area.

Diagram 13 illustrates the guard-to-corner option.

G¹ passes to F³ and goes outside F³ to the corner. F³ feeds G¹ on the baseline and cuts through between 5 and 1, looking for a return pass on the give-and-go. If F³ is not open on his cut, 5 times his move from the high post. If F³ does not receive the give-and-go return pass, 5 rolls down to the baseline and sets a screen on G¹, who has the ball. The entire right side of the floor is open for the two-on-two screening situation for 5 and 1. After 5 sets the screen on G¹, G¹ dribbles over the top of the screen for a jump shot.

If G¹ is not open and a switch occurs, then 5 will be open on the roll. We have also created a mismatch situation with a post man and

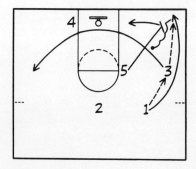

Diagram 13

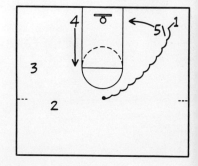

Diagram 14

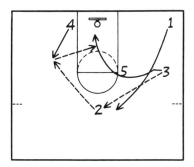

Diagram 15

a guard involved. If 5 is open on the roll, then he will have a guard defending him on the roll. This big man–little man option is an excellent method of creating a mismatch whenever you encounter a team with small defensive guards.

Diagram 14 illustrates the rotation of the guard-to-corner option.

F^3 clears through and sets up at a strong-side forward. 4 moves up to the high-post position, 2 moves over to the strong-side guard, 1 comes over the screen and becomes the weak-side guard, and 5 sets up at the low-post position after his roll to the goal.

In Diagram 15 we see the second option of the guard-to-corner series. In some instances, F^3 will encounter an overplay by the defense on the guard (G^1) after his cut to the baseline and will not allow us to pass to him. In this situation, F^3 hits back to the weak-side guard (G^2); G^2 feeds weak-side forward (F^4), F^3 lines up his defensive man for a cut off of high-post man 5. G^1, whose cut had carried him through to the baseline, comes back out to the back court after F^3 feeds the ball back to the weak side to counteract any overplay on G^2. G^1 fills the weak-side guard position while G^2 has moved over and filled the strong-side guard position. F^3 sets up at the strong-side forward position on the opposite side of the floor after his cut off of high-post man 5. High-post man 5 rolls down the lane after F^3's cut. If F^3 does receive a pass, high-post 5 may be open down the lane. If he is not open, he sets up at the weak-side forward as in Diagram 16.

NOTE: F^4 may first feed F^3 on his high or low cut off of high-post man 5, or feed 5 rolling down the lane.

The third option of the guard-to-corner series is illustrated in Diagram 17. F^3 has the ball, and the Flip-Flop has rotated or turned over to the opposite side of the floor.

F^3 feeds back out to G^2, who feeds G^1, and weak-side forward 5 comes up fast and sets a screen at the foul lane extended on G^1. G^1 comes over the top of the screen for a jump shot or a pass to 5 on the roll. If both G^1 or 5 are covered, then the high-post man 4 rolls across the lane after 5 has rolled under the basket to the opposite side of the lane. G^1 feeds 4 on the side of the lane, and they work a two-on-two big man–little man situation.

Diagram 18 illustrates the rotation of the third option of the guard-to-corner series.

F^3 holds his position at the strong-side forward; G^2 holds his position at the strong-side guard; F^5, who set the initial screen on

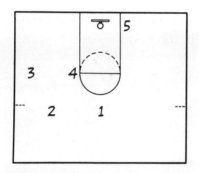

Diagram 16

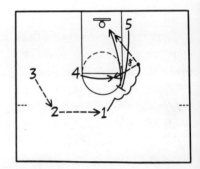

Diagram 17

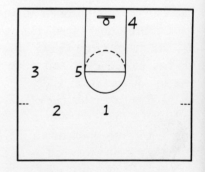

Diagram 18

G^1, rolls under the basket and then moves out high to fill the high-post position of 4, who has moved across the lane for the two-on-two situation with G^1. If 4 is not open for a shot, then he rolls low and assumes the weak-side forward position. G^1 goes back out to the top and fills the weak-side guard position.

After this option is completed, the offense is ready to flow back to the opposite side of the floor. You will notice the interchanging of the two post men (high-post/weak-side forward). These options will be extremely beneficial to any coach who has a couple of big pivot men he does not want to revolve outside into the perimeter rotation. This pattern offers the coach good movement of his post men and at the same time leaves them in advantageous rebounding position.

Post Exchange Option

The post exchange is another option of the guard-to-forward initiation series. This option is keyed by a pass from G^1 to F^3 and an interchange between G^1 and G^2. When high-post man 5 sees the interchange between the guards, he rolls down the lane and sets a screen on the weak-side forward. Diagrams 19A and 19B illustrate the post exchange between F^4 and high-post 5. F^4 can either go over the top or take the baseline cut, according to the position of his defensive man. Diagram 19A illustrates the top cut by F^4.

If the defense switches the screener, 5 will roll the opposite route

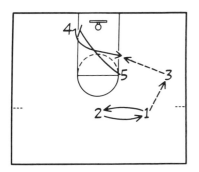

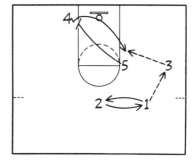

Diagram 19A   *Diagram 19B*

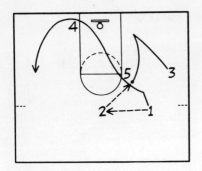
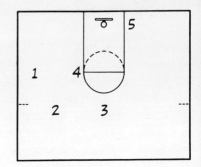

Diagram 20   *Diagram 21*

of F⁴'s cut. Diagram 19B illustrates F⁴'s baseline route off the post interchange. This option will be extremely effective for those coaches who have their offensive scoring concentrated inside the pivot area.

The post exchange can be set any time the post men are overplayed and have become static. The post exchange is an excellent option to run in setting up another option. It can be used when initiating other options in the Flip-Flop and helps to make them more effective. It can also be utilized when another option is completed and no shot has been taken. This simple rotation of the pivot men tends to loosen up the middle area and keeps the defensive pivot men rotating.

GUARD-TO-GUARD INITIATION

The guard-to-guard series plays an important role in the Flip-Flop Offense. It offers a countermove against a strong, aggressive defensive overplay of the forwards, which every coach will encounter during the course of a season.

The guard-to-guard option does not need to be keyed verbally but is recognized by a pass from G^1 to G^2 and a cut by G^1. G^1 passes to G^2 and cuts hard off high-post man 5. F^3 takes his man on a hard cut down to the baseline behind high-post 5 as if he is clearing out to the other side of the floor. He then cuts back directly over the top of high-post man 5, rubbing his defensive man off on him, and receives a pass from G^2 for a jump shot. If he receives the pass and cannot get a shot, he has a two-on-two situation with 5 (Diagram 20).

NOTE: F^3 must time his cut so he will be coming over the top of high-post 5 as G^1 is cutting down the three-second lane. If F^3 cannot find an open shot, the rotation for this option is shown in Diagram 21.

G^1, after his cut, sets up as the strong-side forward on the opposite side of the floor. Low-post 4 moves up to fill the high-post position. G^2 moves over and fills the strong-side guard position. F^3 moves out to the weak-side guard spot, and 5 moves down to the weak-side forward spot.

In Diagram 22, we see the second option of the guard-to-guard initiation. G^1 has passed to G^2 and cut off of high-post 5; F^3 makes his baseline move and comes over the top of high-post 5. If G^2 is unable to feed F^3 as his defensive man has fought over the screen, G^2 instead feeds F^4 as he moves up the lane to meet the pass. As F^4 receives the ball, F^3 cuts hard off of high-post man 5's screen, either taking the top cut or the baseline cut. F^4 feeds him if he is open or has the defensive man on his back. If a switch occurs, high-post 5 rolls the opposite way for a pass.

Diagram 23 illustrates the rotation of the second option of the guard-to-guard initiation.

In this option, G^1, after he sets up initially at the forward position, momentarily is shoved out to the strong-side guard position. F^3, after his cut, sets up as the strong-side forward, 4 moves up to the high post, 5 rolls to the low post, and G^2 moves over to the weak-side guard.

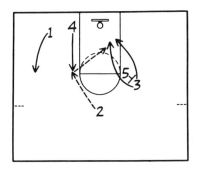

Diagram 22

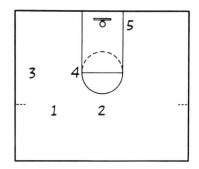

Diagram 23

Diagram 24A shows G¹'s cut off the high-post man after the guard-to-guard initiation. Notice he cuts away from F³, down the lane, and around low-post man 4. This route is the quickest one and enables the offense to start its movement opening up the high-post area.

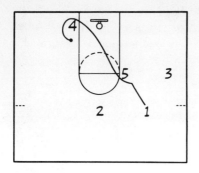

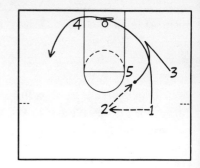

Diagram 24A   *Diagram 24B*

Diagram 24B illustrates the route G¹ takes if F³ is being guarded closely or by a strong defensive player. G¹, after his pass to G², makes a sharp cut between high-post 5 and F³. F³ uses G¹ and high-post 5 as a double screen which offers the defensive man more difficulty in stopping this high-post screen off the ball. G¹'s rotation is the same regardless of his routes, as illustrated in 24A or 24B.

After the guard-to-guard series has been run a few times against a tight man-to-man defense, the defensive guard will not follow G¹ all the way through his cutting route. Rather, he will sag or float in the lane and try to protect the lane area. In Diagram 24C, we see a counter-option for this defensive move. As G¹ makes his pass to G² and cuts the lane, as soon as he sees his defensive man sagging away from him, he calls out "sag" to G². He then comes around weak-side forward 4, who has spread out and formed a screen for G¹ at the low post, and G² feeds G¹ behind this screen for a short jump shot.

THE GUARD-TO-WEAK-SIDE FORWARD INITIATION

The success of an offense is highly dependent upon its ability to be run equally as well from the right as from the left side of the floor. An offense that can only be initiated from the strong side of the floor is as limited as a basketball player that can only go to his right on the dribble.

The Flip-Flop Offense is as effective in its initiation to the weak

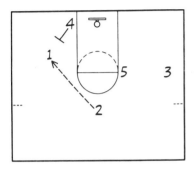

Diagram 24C

side as the strong side.

Diagram 25 illustrates the first option of the guard-to-weak-side series. G^2 passes to F^4 and cuts hard on a give-and-go cut down the lane. G^2's cut will determine the option that will be run, depending upon whether or not he goes inside or outside of F^4. If G^2 is open on his inside cut, F^4 will feed him for the driving lay-up.

If G^2 is not open on his cut, then you will notice he has opened up the weak-side area for a one-on-one or a two-on-two situation.

In Diagram 26A, high-post 5 waits until 2 is out of F^4's passing range and then comes across and sets a screen on F^4's defensive man just outside the three-second lane. F^4 comes over the top of the screen for a jump shot or, in case there is no switch, a drive to the basket for a lay-up. If the defense switches, F^4 will feed high-post 5 on the roll to the basket. The lower F^4 can receive the ball, the more effective high-post 5's screen will be. Also, F^4 will have more floor area to operate away from the sagging defensive men.

This option is another post-man option in the Flip-Flop that a coach with either one or two good pivot men in his line-up can utilize.

In the event that F^4 does not have a shot coming over the top of F^5, then the second-guard option is available with G^1 as the second

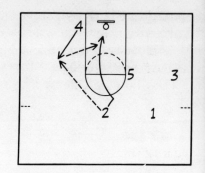

Diagram 25

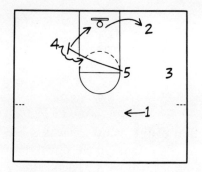

Diagram 26A

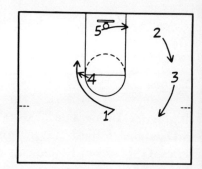

Diagram 26B

guard (Diagram 26B). This also is a big man–little man situation and will create a mismatch in the event the defense switches on this movement.

The rotation on this pattern is shown in Diagram 27. G^2, who made the first pass to F^4 to start the pattern, went through and set up momentarily on the opposite side of the floor, and then moved out to fill F^3's vacated spot after F^3 moved out to replace the guard G^1, who had run the second-guard option. High-post 5 sets his screen on F^4 and then rolls. If he does not receive the ball, he sets up at the high post on the opposite side of the floor. F^4 sets and remains the weak-side forward on the same side of the floor. G^1, if he is not open on the second-guard option, turns back out and sets up at the weak-side guard position.

NOTE: If the weak-side option is run through and no shot is

available, F^4 can pass the ball back out to G^3, who can initiate the pattern on the strong side as shown in Diagram 28.

The strength of the Flip-Flop is its continuous flow from one side of the floor to the other.

Outside Cut

We have seen in Diagrams 25–28 the inside cut options of the guard-to-weak-side forward pattern. Now let us look at the outside cut on the weak-side pattern (Diagram 29).

G^2 passes to F^4 and cuts outside and receives a hand-off from F^4. F^4 rolls to the basket and, in case of a switch, looks for a pass on the roll. He continues under and sets up beside high-post 5, forming a double screen at the edge of the lane. F^3 lines his man up for a cut

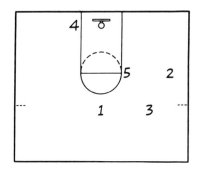

Diagram 27

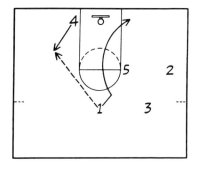

Diagram 28

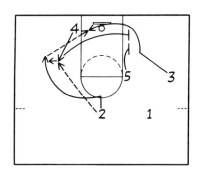

Diagram 29

off of F^4 and F^5. He can take either the top route or the baseline route on his cut. G^2 looks to feed F^3, if possible, for the crip or the short jump shot. If F^3 is not open, he sets up on the baseline. G^2 can either feed F^3 at the stationary low-post position where he has set himself up, or he can feed back outside to G^1 and start the second phase of the option.

NOTE: If F^3 is a good one-on-one basketball player, this option will create a good one-on-one situation for him on the low post.

If the offense cannot obtain a good shot from this pattern, F^4 starts the second phase of the guard-to-weak-side option. F^2 passes out to G^1. G^1 then looks to F^4, who steps out behind high-post 5 for a jump shot. This pattern has been a very effective weapon against sagging defenses, which, in most cases, will be sagging in the lane toward F^3, who has set up at the low-post position. F^4 should receive the pass directly behind high-post 5, where he will be open for a short-range jump shot (Diagram 30).

Diagram 31 shows a countermove for this pattern if F^4 is not open behind high-post 5's screen and cannot receive a pass from G^1. G^1 then looks to F^3 on the baseline, who moves up the lane to receive a pass from G^1. F^3 then looks to pass to F^4 as he cuts off high-post 5, either down the lane or on a back door cut.

NOTE: F^3 is responsible for rubbing his defensive man off on high-post 5 on his cut.

Rotation: F^4, after his cut, sets up at the strong-side forward. F^3 has established a high-post position. G^2 circles out and becomes the strong-side guard; G^1 sets up at the weak-side guard; 5 moves down the lane and sets up at the weak-side forward position.

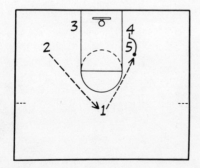

Diagram 30

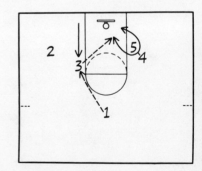

Diagram 31

The Flip-Flop Offense can be initiated from any player position and from any area of the floor. Many offenses can only be initiated or started by a guard-to-a-forward pass and cut to the basket. These offenses are too stereotyped in their offensive movement to be successful against the better basketball teams. Conversely, flexibility of the Flip-Flop Offense, in the initiation of the pattern, makes it impossible for the defense to concentrate on any particular player or area of the floor.

The Flip-Flop Offense thrives against the pressure defenses employed by many modern teams. The releases and maneuvers a team must have to combat this pressure are easily incorporated into the player movement of the Flip-Flop patterns. On numerous occasions, whenever playing against pressure defenses, the release maneuvers we have utilized to combat pressure have resulted in lay-up baskets. However, in most instances, these release maneuvers help us mainly to initiate the offense and flow into our patterns.

The Flip-Flop initiations can be keyed either verbally or by the position of the ball and the cutting routes of the passers. The use of verbal keys when first installing the Flip-Flop in preseason practice sessions will simplify the learning process for the players. By using the position of the ball and the cutting routes of the passer for keying the Flip-Flop, the options of the offense will be disguised better, and the defense will have more difficulty recognizing these keys. There are several factors that can determine the type of keys to use with the Flip-Flop, such as experience of the players, the coach's philosophy, and the level of competition.

The Flip-Flop options we have discussed in this chapter are employed against man-to-man defenses. In Chapter 2, we shall discuss the Flip-Flop versus the pressure defenses.

2

The Flip-Flop Offense Versus the Pressure Defenses

If an offense is going to be successful against modern pressure defenses, it must have releases or safety valves, to go to in times of emergencies. Many basketball games have been won by teams whose personnel have been far inferior to other teams by applying pressure to their guards. A common practice today is to apply tight man-to-man pressure to the opposing team's guards at either half-court or full-court. This strategy is extremely effective in most cases; on the other hand, it can also be disastrous against an offense that thrives against pressure and is practiced daily against pressure, an important practice element a lot of coaches on both the high school and college level overlook. If you decide to run the Flip-Flop or utilize any options in your offense, you should run these options each day in practice against both half- and full-court pressure.

In the diagrams that follow, we are going to illustrate some of the basic countermoves of the Flip-Flop against pressure man-to-man defenses. When encountering a pressure defense with the Flip-Flop, we try to set up one-on-one situations for our strongest offensive players. These situations will be numerous as the defense is spread out over the court when exerting pressure upon the offense. When the defensive player overcommits himself or misses a defensive slide in a pressure situation, it will in most cases result in a field goal for the offense.

GUARD "HOOK-BACK"

The first countermove is the guard "hook-back." This move can be used against either half-court or full-court pressure on the guards. Diagram 32 illustrates the "hook-back" against half-court pressure. You will notice that G^1 has performed the "hook-back"; he has carried his defensive man through and then hooked back. In doing this he has opened up his vacated area for G^2 to come on the dribble and start the offense. This move has also given G^2 more floor area to operate one-on-one when he is being pressured tightly from the half-court area. Either G^2 or G^1 can perform the "hook-back" depending on who has possession of the ball. The guard without the ball is always the "hook-back" man.

This move is also very effective against a full-court, man-to-man press. Diagram 33 illustrates the "hook-back" in a full-court situation.

HIGH-POST RELEASE

The high-post man is the "hub" of the Flip-Flop Offense. The utilization of the high post when encountering pressure defenses is extremely important. The high-post man should be drilled to come high to receive a pass when the guards are encountering pressure from the defense (Diagram 34). Upon receiving the pass from a

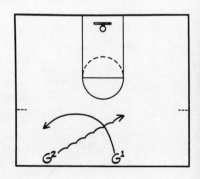

Diagram 32

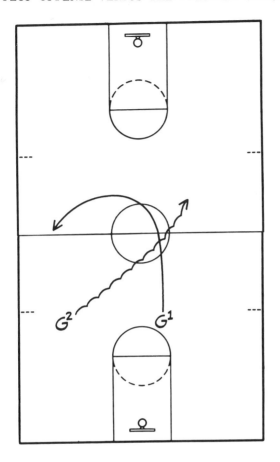

Diagram 33

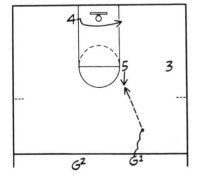

Diagram 34

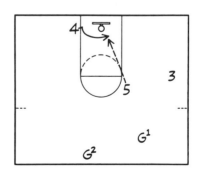

Diagram 35

guard, the high-post man turns and "faces up" to the basket. By this we mean he squares his head and shoulders to the basket. This move puts him in the "triple threat" position—he can either shoot, pass or dribble. His first option after "facing up" is to look for F^4, the low-post man coming across the lane, who has maneuvered his defensive man into trailing him across the lane.

This develops into a perfect two-on-two situation for our inside men. The pressure defense is spread and thus gives our offensive post men a wide area inside in which they can operate effectively (Diagram 35).

His next option is, after a quick look for F^4 coming across the lane, to drive toward F^4's vacated spot on a one-on-one situation. F^4 has performed a clear-out when coming across the lane and has given high-post man 5 a vacated area in which to maneuver his defensive man (Diagram 36).

THE "CLEAR-OUT"

The "clear-out" is one of the most widely used offensive moves in modern basketball. There are few teams, regardless of the offensive system they employ, that will not clear out against a pressure defense.

A "clear-out" occurs when an offensive player purposely vacates his floor position near the ball to enable the player with the ball to operate more efficiently. This move gives the player with the ball more floor area in which to operate against the defense in a one-on-one situation.

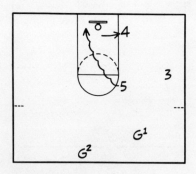

Diagram 36

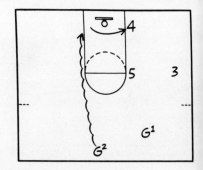

Diagram 37

Forward Clear-Out

The first clear-out situation we shall discuss is a forward clear-out. This is an effective move when the guards are receiving pressure from the defense at mid-court. The offensive guard will maneuver his defensive man into the cleared area, thus increasing the area the defensive man has to cover and eliminating a possible double-team situation.

Diagram 37 illustrates the forward clear-out option. F^4 has cleared out to the other side of the foul lane. You will notice he has stopped directly underneath the goal on the opposite side of the lane. This is an important move on the part of F^4 (the clearing forward). If his defensive man does not follow him all the way on his clear-out route, then he will be open under the basket in perfect scoring position. When clearing out, F^4 should go full speed to the opposite baseline. This will give G^2 more time to operate and leaves the vacated area completely open when he starts his drive.

NOTE: The clear-out will be far more effective if F^4 will clear on his own without a verbal or hand signal from G^2. A signal from G^2 will alert the defensive guard on him and cause him to overplay the cleared-out area while F^4 is in the process of clearing out.

To add to the effectiveness of the clear-out, F^4 should time his clear-out while G^2 is still dribbling and his defensive man is back-pedaling. The ideal time for F^4 to start his clear-out is when G^2 is one or two steps across half-court. This timing will give the offensive guard G^2 the advantage, as he has his forward momentum going with his weight on his toes, whereas the defensive guard is back-pedaling with his weight shifted to his heels.

Guard Clear-Out

The second clear-out situation is the guard clear-out. This move may be initiated by both guards and operated on whichever side of the floor they decide to run it to, according to where the defensive pressure is placed.

Diagram 38 illustrates a guard clear-out after the guard-to-forward pass has been made. G^1 passes to F^3 and goes directly away from F^3, opening up the area outside the foul lane extended for F^3 to operate if he decides to rub his man off high-post man 5.

Remember that G^1's cut on his clear-out route should be a sharp, quick cut away from the forward. If G^1's defensive man does not follow him, and he sags in the lane as illustrated in Diagram 39, G^1 immediately alters his route and cuts underneath the basket for a lay-up via the back door route.

Many times the defensive man on clear-outs will follow the offensive guard the first two or three steps and then sag in the lane and try to congest the scoring area. It is important that G^1, after his initial cut on his clear-out, checks his defensive man, and if he is sagging in the lane, he cuts directly under the basket. If F^3's offensive movement is stalled and he is unable to feed G^1 underneath the basket, then G^1 cuts back out and balances up at his original floor position.

High Post Clear-Out

The third clear-out option is the high post clear-out. Whenever the Flip-Flop experiences strong defensive post play and pressure from the inside defensive men, the post man will clear away from the ball (Diagram 40).

This clear-out will open up the entire lane area and enable the

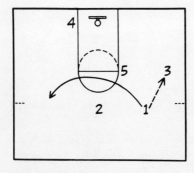

Diagram 38

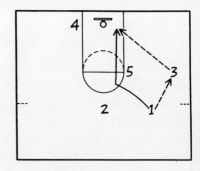

Diagram 39

offensive forward to operate one-on-one.

NOTE: After F³ has received the ball, if he wants to clear the post man away, he puts the ball above his head. This is the key for the high-post man to clear across the lane.

When utilizing the high post clear-out in the Flip-Flop, if there is no offensive opportunity available after the clear-out, then we simply flip the offense over to the other side of the floor (Diagram 41).

Notice that when high-post man 5 has cleared across the lane, F⁴ comes high and establishes a strong-side forward position. G² moves to a strong-side guard position. F³ goes to a weak-side forward position and 1 sets up at a weak-side guard position.

The Double Clear-Out

From time to time during a game when we are relying heavily on clear-outs against a strong defensive team, we will use double clear-outs. A double clear-out results when two offensive players clear out and move away from the ball.

Diagram 42 illustrates our guard-forward double clear-out for our high-post man. F³ has cleared out to the opposite side of the floor. G¹ passes to G² and also clears to the opposite side of floor. G²

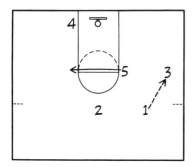

Diagram 40

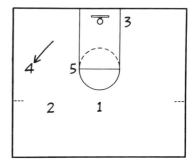

Diagram 41

feeds high-post man 5, and he works on his defensive man in a one-on-one situation. This clear-out should be used often in the Flip-Flop if you have a strong offensive post man. It is an excellent method of feeding the pivot, for you have eliminated the "sag" by clearing F^3 and G^1. We will key this double clear-out with a bounce pass from G^1 to G^2—this is an excellent key because we do not normally use a bounce pass when passing from a guard to a guard.

Diagram 43 illustrates the turnover from the guard-forward double-clear option.

F^3 clears and sets up at the strong-side forward; weak-side forward 4 becomes high-post 4; high-post 5 becomes weak-side forward; G^1 clears to strong-side guard and G^2 becomes weak-side guard.

In Diagram 44 we see a guard-forward double clear-out that sets up an offensive guard for a drive to the basket. This is an excellent option to incorporate in the Flip-Flop if you have guards who can take the ball to the basket on the dribble.

G^2 passes to G^1 and clears out down the lane. Weak-side forward 4 clears across the lane to the opposite side. G^1, after receiving a

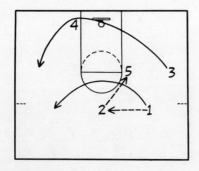

Diagram 42

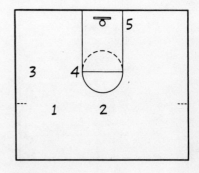

Diagram 43

pass from G^2, dribbles to the weak side and drives hard to the cleared-out area of the court. We use the bounce pass again as a key for this double clear-out with G^2 bounce passing to G^1 and running a clear-out route; weak-side forward 4, upon seeing G^2 clear across the key, also clears across the lane to open up the area for G^1's drive to the basket.

Diagram 45 illustrates the turnover on this double-clear option. G^2 passes to G^1, clears down the lane, and sets up at strong-side guard position. Weak-side forward 4, after his clear across the lane, moves up and sets at the high post. High-post man 5 rolls down and establishes a low-post position. G^1, after his one-on-one maneuver, sets up at the weak-side guard.

The key to this particular double clear-out occurs when it is evident that 4 has cleared G^1 and cannot operate against his defensive man one-on-one, so he passes to G^2 and clears out down the lane, thus setting G^2 up to try a one-on-one situation.

The clear-out and double clear-out options in the Flip-Flop Offense enable a team to utilize their best offensive basketball players. These options set up one-on-one situations. They are free-lance

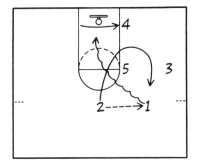

Diagram 44

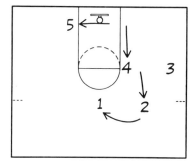

Diagram 45

options that allow the coach to take advantage of his best offensive basketball players and utilize them in situations against pressure defenses. Too often coaches use a restricted, disciplined type of offense that does not set up free-lance situations. The clear-out is an excellent method of offensing the man-to-man pressure defenses, either half-court or full-court.

THE FLIP-FLOP VERSUS THE ZONE PRESSURE DEFENSES

Since the innovation of the zone press, the zone pressure defenses have become increasingly popular. The zone press has become a devastating defensive weapon capable of completely demolishing the offensive system that is not prepared to meet and counter the double-team situations.

The Flip-Flop Offense, by employing a few minor adjustments, can easily counteract zone pressure double-teams and turn them into scoring opportunities for the offense.

OFFENSING THE FULL-COURT ZONE PRESSURE DEFENSES

The basic floor alignment in offensing full-court zone pressure defenses is basically the same as the half-court Flip-Flop alignment. Diagram 46 illustrates the initial floor alignment of the press offense. G^2 is out-of-bounds with the basketball; G^1 is the in-bounds guard; F^3 is the strong-side forward and is lined up in the back court with the guards. 4 is the middle man and is constantly button-hooking up and back, working to get open. 5 is the weak-side forward and goes deep, looking for the possible long pass and easy basket.

Diagram 47 illustrates the in-bounds pass and the beginning of our press offense. Out-of-bounds guard G^2 passes in-bounds to G^1; G^2, after passing, steps in-bounds but stays at least two steps behind G^1 for a possible return pass; this position offers G^1 a much better return passing angle in the event he is double-teamed. G^1 looks to F^3, who has button-hooked upcourt and back, for a possible pass if he has worked himself open. He feeds F^3; F^3 then attempts to advance the ball or feed middle man 4, who is working to get open. If neither of these options is available, and in most cases against a strong press neither of them will be successful, then F^3 can feed back to G^1.

Diagram 48 illustrates the second phase of our zone press offense. Notice that F^3 has the ball and cannot find an opening in the press; consequently, he quickly passes back to G^1 and goes toward the goal and sets up as the deep man. F^5, upon seeing F^3's return pass to G^1, starts to return quickly to the strong-side forward position in the back court. G^1 passes to G^2, who quickly dribbles, looking for an opening to feed F^5. F^5, upon receiving the pass from G^2, can advance the ball himself or feed middle man 4, who has maneuvered himself open in the middle of the press.

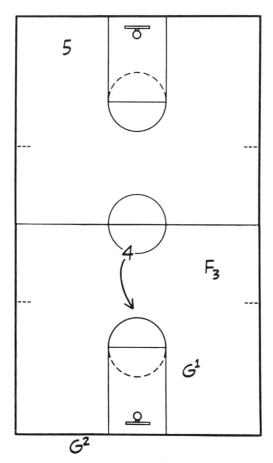

Diagram 46

Diagram 49 illustrates the floor position of the players at the conclusion of our press pattern. Notice we have flip-flopped our offense over to the left side of the court after beginning our pattern on the right side.

This is an excellent offensive pattern against any full-court zone pressure defense.

OFFENSING THE HALF-COURT ZONE PRESSURE DEFENSES

Half-court zone pressure defenses have become increasingly popular and are a constant threat to a pattern type of basketball team.

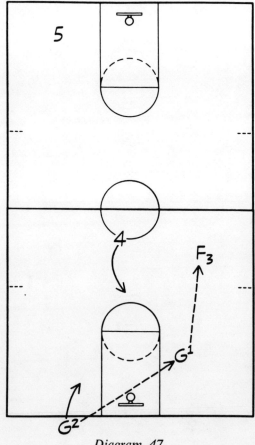

Diagram 47

We will counter these defenses most of the time with our high-post man coming high and attempting to feed into the middle of the press. However, we do have definite options designed to combat these half-court zone pressure defenses.

If the defense is using a one-guard front, as in a 1-3-1, 1-2-2, 1-2-1-1, etc., we will offense this defense with a two-guard offensive front and attempt to make the point defensive man commit himself as shown in Diagram 50.

After the defensive guard has made a definite commitment, the offensive guard will pass the ball to the free guard, and he takes the ball into the gap of the defense (Diagram 51).

Notice G^2 has the ball now, and his first passing option is to feed

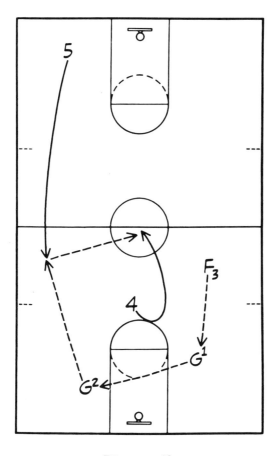

Diagram 48

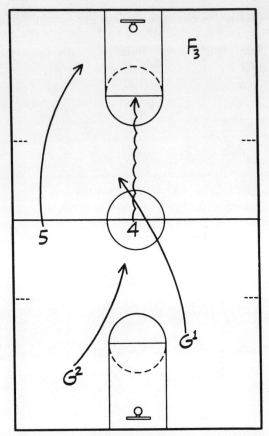

Diagram 49

the middle high-post man 5. High-post 5, upon receiving the ball, faces up to the basket and feeds the weak-side forward under the basket.

Whenever the defense comes at us with a two-guard front, we instruct our guards to maintain their floor balance and take the ball head on into the defensive guards instead of splitting them. This maneuver makes it harder for the defensive guards to double-team out front because it keeps them spread. We will instruct the forward, upon seeing the guards penetrate the defense, to go low to the baseline (Diagram 52).

The offensive guard with the ball (G²) will look to the middle of the press for the open man. 5 has rolled down the lane and set up low and away. The offensive forward opposite the ball flashes the middle of the press for the pass. Upon receiving the ball, he feeds high-post 5 on the baseline (Diagram 53).

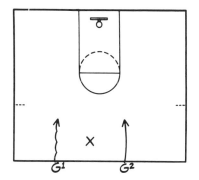

Diagram 50

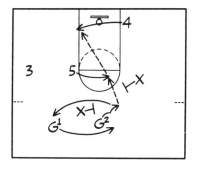

Diagram 51

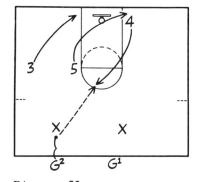

Diagram 52

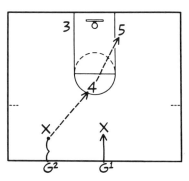

Diagram 53

If he is unable to feed the baseline, he looks to the wing and feeds G^2, who has moved down on the weak-side wing for the shot (Diagram 54).

The important thing to remember in offensing half-court zone pressure defenses is that you must penetrate the perimeter of the defense and that you must go first to the strong side, then back to the weak side with the basketball. Let me emphasize how important it is for the offensive guards to maintain their poise at all times. The pressure defenses are extremely vulnerable to the team that maintains its poise and has a planned pattern of attack.

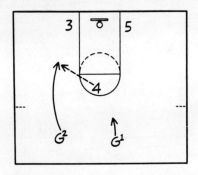

Diagram 54

3

The Flip-Flop Versus the Zone Defenses

The Flip-Flop Offense is capable of offensing any zone defense effectively by making only a few minor adjustments. The basic floor positions are the same when initiating the Flip-Flop against the man-to-man or the zone defenses. The ability of the Flip-Flop to operate effectively against a variety of defenses is probably its most outstanding characteristic. Many times, in modern basketball, a team will have several different offenses to be used against specific defenses. This system only tends to confuse the players and minimizes confidence in their offense when one of these particular offenses stalls after an opponent makes a defensive adjustment or change.

The Flip-Flop, on the other hand, tends to exert tremendous pressure on the defense and is poised and ready to react to any defensive adjustments or changes.

Another advantage in installing the Flip-Flop Offense is practical utilization of practice time during the week. Instead of spending practice time developing three or four different offenses to combat the different defenses, the coach can spend his offensive time allotment in practice on the Flip-Flop exclusively, thus leaving himself more practice time for the basic offensive fundamentals and other important areas of the game.

The Flip-Flop's ability to function against different defenses will greatly increase the players' confidence in their offense and in their team. Any offense, in order to be effective, must have the confidence of the players and the coaching staff.

When our ball club is to encounter a team that uses a zone defense, we first show them the weak spots in the zone they will meet and teach them to look forward to playing against a zone defense. This indoctrination of our players is essential, just as the mental conditioning of our athletes is as important as the physical conditioning.

THE FLIP-FLOP ZONE OFFENSE

The Flip-Flop, when operating against a zone, relies upon constant player movement and movement of the ball, the theory of the zone offense being to keep the defense continually adjusting to cutters and the movement of the ball. When offensing a zone defense, we will initiate our zone attack from the Flip-Flop, rotate into a 1-3-1, and then back into a Flip-Flop overload formation.

The first option of the zone offense which we are going to discuss is the strong-side guard to the corner.

THE STRONG-SIDE GUARD TO THE CORNER OPTION

The first option of our Flip-Flop zone attack is the strong-side guard to the corner (Diagram 55). G^1 has passed the ball to F^3 (strong-side forward) and started his inside cut instead of going away from the ball as in our man-to-man initiation of the Flip-Flop. He cuts to the corner and sets up on the baseline. (Notice that the X in Diagram 55 is the exact position on the baseline at which he sets up after his cut.)

If the zone fails to adjust after G^1's cut and G^1 is open on the baseline after his cut, then F^3 will pass to him for a short jump shot. (NOTE: G^1's initial cut is the same as in the strong-side guard to forward initiation of the man-to-man Flip-Flop Offense.) G^1's initial cut is an important phase of our zone attack. The initial routes of the cutters are the same as in the Flip-Flop man-to-man attack. In the event a team attempts to change defenses on us on the floor by switching from a man-to-man to a zone as some modern teams do, G^1 can simply alter his route and cut to the baseline instead of going away from the ball where he is ready to offense the zone. G^1 will check his defensive man on his cut through the defense. If he does not follow him through, it is a zone defense and he takes the baseline route. On the other hand, if his defensive man does go with him, he takes him away from F^3 and initiates the Flip-Flop man-to-man offense. This simple keying system cuts down on offensive confusion whenever a team attempts to change defenses on the floor. Many times, whenever one team attempts quick defensive changes against another team, the offensive team has to regroup their offense after each defensive change. If an offense is not flexible enough to adjust automatically as the Flip-Flop is able to do, then you are in for trouble against a smart defensive ball club.

After G^1's cut to the baseline, high-post 5 checks the defensive baseline man when he moves out to cover G^1. Then he rolls down the lane and will be open for a pass from either F^3 or G^1 (Diagram 56). If high-post 5 is not open on his roll down the lane, then he sets up on the baseline at the edge of the foul lane.

You will note that G^1, F^3, and high-post 5 have set up an offensive triangle in offensing the zone defense. This triangle sets up an

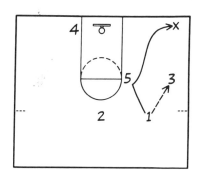

Diagram 55

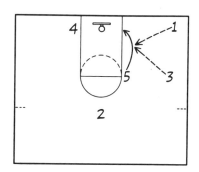

Diagram 56

overload on one side of the floor and will force the defense to adjust.

F^3 has possession of the ball and is in a triple-threat position. He can shoot; pass to G¹, who has cut through the defense; or pass to high-post 5, who has rolled down to the baseline and set up there. In the event F³ passes to G¹ on the baseline, he cuts through the zone looking for a return pass (Diagram 57).

F³ has passed the ball to G¹ on the baseline and cut through, setting up on the opposite wing position. G¹ dribbles out to the wing position where he passes the ball back to G² on the point.

G² passes the ball over to F³ on the weak-side wing position. 5, who is set up on the opposite baseline, rolls across the lane following the flow of the ball and around a screen set by 4. 4 does not break up to the high-post position on this pattern; he holds his position on the baseline. F³ has the alternative of passing either to 5 for a jump shot behind 4's screen or inside to 4, who will be open if the defense elects to overplay 5.

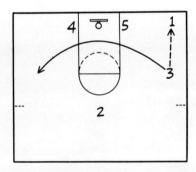

Diagram 57

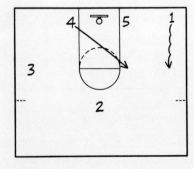

Diagram 58A

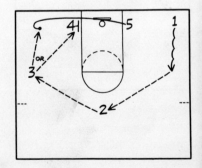

Diagram 58B

NOTE: This is an excellent option for a post man who possesses a good short-range jump shot. The first few times we utilized this pattern we found 5 to be open for a jump shot. Then, when the defense contained 5, we took the ball inside to 4.

The rebounding responsibilities are as follows: 5 rebounds the strong side, 4 covers the lane area of the board, and 1 is the weak-side rebounder.

If F^3 is not open for a return pass on his cut, he continues through the zone and sets up on the wing on the other side of the floor. G^1, if unable to feed F^3, dribbles out quickly and fills his vacated wing position. As G^1 is in the process of dribbling out and filling F^3's vacated floor position, the defense has sagged to defense F^3's cut through the zone. When G^1 has dribbled out to fill the vacated guard position, the zone will flex out to defend against G^1. Low-post man 4 (who has set up on the opposite baseline at the edge of the key) times his move, and when the zone flexes out to cover G^1, he cuts up through the heart of the lane to the high-post area (Diagram 58A).

NOTE: G^1 passes to low-post 4 in the center of the lane for a short jump shot. 4 will be open on many occasions for a short-range jump shot in the heart of the zone defense. When the shot is taken, 3 rebounds the weak side of the board, 5 has established rebounding position on the strong side, and 4 follows his shot by rebounding the lane area.

Diagram 58B illustrates an excellent screening option off of this particular pattern that we have utilized on various occasions against match-up zones and combination defenses. This particular option has offered us excellent inside scoring opportunities and openings on the weak-side baseline.

The Flip-Flop has rotated into a 1-3-1 offensive alignment. We have flooded the center area of the zone with the rotation of 4 and 5. If 4 is not open after his cut to the high post, then 1 passes out to 2, follows his pass outside, and we regroup back into the Flip-Flop overload formation on the opposite side of the floor (Diagram 59).

We have now rotated from the 1-3-1 formation back into the Flip-Flop floor alignment and are now ready to initiate our Flip-Flop zone attack again. 3 remains in his position and is now the strong-side forward; 4 moves across the lane and sets up a high-post position; 5 remains on the baseline and is the weak-side forward;

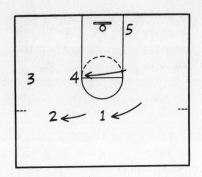

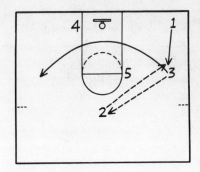

Diagram 59   *Diagram 60*

2 moves over into a strong-side guard position and sets up at weak-side guard position.

NOTE: We have moved from a 1-3-1 formation back into an overload Flip-Flop formation, and from the Flip-Flop formation we can start our penetration cuts again.

If G^1 is not open on the baseline and F^3 cannot pass him the ball, then F^3 passes out to the "point" guard (G^2) and runs the same cutting route through the zone as he would run when he passes the ball down to G^1 on the baseline. After F^3's cut, G^1 moves up and fills the vacated wing position (Diagram 60).

In many instances, G^1 will be open after he fills the wing position for a pass from G^2 and a jump shot. A very important teaching point is that G^1 times his movement up to the wing position so as to be open while the zone is sagging inside to help check F^3's cut through the zone. If G^1 takes the shot after filling the wing position, then 4 rebounds the lane area, 5 the strong side of the board, and 3 is the weak-side rebounder. This is a very effective option against a zone defense that body-checks all cutters. The defense will find it almost impossible to body-check F^3 on his cut through the zone and then react in time to defend against G^1, who has filled the vacated wing position for the jump shot.

The Flip-Flop has now flowed into a 1-3-1 formation, and by movement of the ball around the perimeter of the zone and by exploring the high-post and baseline areas with the 1-3-1 alignment, we can obtain good shots against the zone defenses.

If we are unable to obtain a good shot from the 1-3-1 alignment, we can rotate back into the Flip-Flop and attack the zone again from a two-guard front alignment (Diagram 61).

NOTE: 4 has moved up to the high-post position, 5 has gone to the low-post position, 3 has set up at the strong-side forward, 1 and 2 have filled the guard spots.

THE GUARD SHALLOW CUT ZONE OPTION

The guard shallow cut is the second initiation pattern of the Flip-Flop zone offense. In this pattern, the strong-side guard, in initiating the offense, moves down the lane on a shallow cut after passing to G^2 and fills the wing position on the weak side (Diagram 62).

Strong-side guard G^1 passes to G^2 and cuts down the lane. G^1's cut is a shallow cut down the lane and he sets up on the wing on the weak side. G^2's first option is to pass to G^1 on the wing for a jump shot. G^1 will often find himself open after his shallow cut for the quick jump shot due to many zones' inability to rotate and defense this guard shallow cut. Many times, after his cut, the defensive man in his area will not move or rotate toward his cut, thus inactivating him and setting G^1 loose on the weak-side wing. If G^1 takes the shot after this shallow guard cut, then 4 rebounds the strong side of the board, 5 covers the lane area, and 3 covers the weak side of the board.

NOTE: Whenever we are in a 1-3-1 offensive set, we will send only three men to the board to rebound. We feel we are vulnerable to the fast break whenever we are in a one-guard front offense,

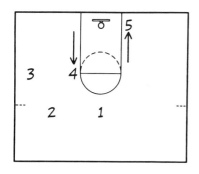

Diagram 61

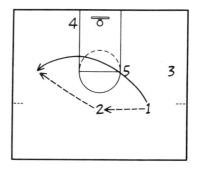

Diagram 62

and we must offset this by pulling a wing man back to balance up the floor after a shot is taken. If a team does not utilize the fast break against us then we will assign a fourth man rebounding responsibilities at the free-throw line.

If G^2 passes to G^1 on the weak-side wing and he is unable to take the shot, then he can run the swing option. You will notice that our offensive floor position is a 1-3-1 alignment, thus enabling us to rotate into the swing option (Diagram 63).

Any time we rotate from the Flip-Flop into a 1-3-1 zone offense, we can run the swing option. This simply means we will send cutters through the zone and rotate our perimeter offensive players.

G^1 passes to low-post 4, who has stepped out on the baseline to receive the pass. G^1 cuts through the heart of the zone, looking for a return pass, and sets up on the wing position on the weak side. 4 dribbles out to the wing position looking for a shot; high-post 5 moves across the lane looking for a shot as 4 is dribbling out to the wing. The zone defense must flex out to defend against 4 as he is dribbling out to the wing position looking for a shot. 3, who has shortened up to the basket, cuts quickly underneath the basket looking for a pass from 4. We have been able to feed 3 who has been wide open underneath the goal on many occasions, or with the defensive man on his back. In the event 3 shoots the ball inside, then 3 is responsible for the strong side of the board himself, 5 rebounds the lane area, and 1 is the weak-side rebounder (Diagram 64).

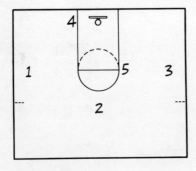

Diagram 63

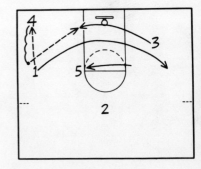

Diagram 64

If 3 is not open on his flash underneath the basket, then he button hooks back to the other side of the lane and sets up a low-post position. We are in a 1-3-1 formation and can attack the zone defense from this alignment or rotate back into our overload Flip-Flop alignment (Diagram 65).

By simple movement of the ball from this 1-3-1 alignment, we should be able to obtain a good high percentage shot. If we are unable to find an opening in the zone, we rotate back in the overload Flip-Flop alignment and attack the zone from a two-guard front alignment (Diagram 66).

NOTE: In rotating back into the Flip-Flop, 2 has moved over and set up at a strong-side guard position, 1 has moved out to the weak-side guard position from the wing, and 3 has set up at a low-post position.

In the event that G^2 is unable to pass the ball to G^1 after his shallow guard cut, he looks to feed the ball to F^3 who has set up at the strong-side forward. The offensive movement is changed somewhat if G^2 elects to go away from G^1 with the ball.

This movement revolves the post men and gives us the inside movement necessary in offensing a zone defense. This post rotation keeps the zone from flexing out and defensing our perimeter jump shots (Diagram 67).

When G^2 has passed to F^3, high-post man 5 executes a straight cut down to an open area on the baseline. If he is open, F^3 passes to him for a jump shot. Low-post man 4 cuts through the heart

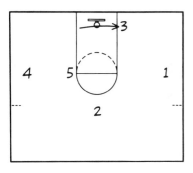

Diagram 65

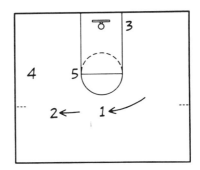

Diagram 66

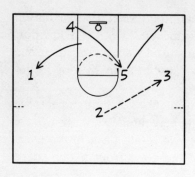

Diagram 67

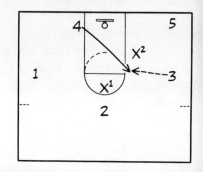

Diagram 68

of the zone looking for a jump shot and sets up at the high-post area which high-post 5 has vacated. Again we instruct low-post 4 to "hunt daylight" in the zone and split the two defensive players. His cut up to the high post should be timed according to the movement of the zone toward high-post 5's cut to the baseline.

Diagram 68 illustrates what we mean by low-post 4 "hunting daylight" in his move to the high post. Low-post 4 will hunt an opening at the gap between the two defensive men X^1 and X^2. This is an important teaching point in your pivot play. Many times the post man takes himself out of the play by stationing himself directly behind a defensive player and the offense is unable to pass to him.

We are now in the 1-3-1 offensive alignment again, and can run the "swing" option. 3 passes the ball to 5 on the baseline and cuts through and sets up at the forward position; 5 passes to 2 and sets up at the low-post position; 4 moves across the lane and sets up at the high post; 1 steps out and sets up at the strong-side guard position; and 2 maintains his guard position (Diagram 69).

NOTE: We have now rotated from the 1-3-1 offensive alignment back into the overload Flip-Flop alignment. In rotating from a one-guard front to a two-guard front, many times we will free a guard for a jump shot at the head of the key. This is due mainly to the zone defense's failure to flex out to cover the offensive player filling the vacated guard position.

THE 1-2-2 ZONE OFFENSE

The 1-2-2 offense is one of the most widely used offensive formations in basketball today. Teams throughout the southeastern area, from the junior high school level up through the college level, have used the 1-2-2 offensive alignment with great success. I first decided to utilize some of the options of the 1-2-2 set at DeKalb County High School a few seasons ago.

I had lost four out of my five starters from my previous year's team that had finished with a fine 17–6 record. We were picked to

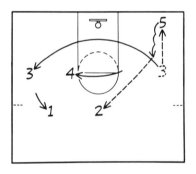

Diagram 69

win seven games, at the most, and this was thought to be an optimistic outlook for the season. We had two good-size post men who could score, and the other three players were good short-to-medium-distance jump shooters. We played a 23-game schedule and about 80 per cent of the high school teams in the area used zone defense as their basic defense. I decided to experiment with a double low-post (1-2-2) alignment against the zones we would face that season. The 1-3-1 and 1-2-2 zone defenses were the defenses we encountered the most from our opponents that year. We compiled an 18–5 overall record, and much of the success of the season, I feel, was due to the 1-2-2 zone offense.

The 1-2-2 offense gives us excellent inside scoring opportunities and excellent scoring opportunities from the wings. In the 1-2-2 zone attack, we will screen the zone defenses. This is unlike the Flip-Flop zone offense that uses movement and cutters to offense the zone defenses. With the conception of the "match-up" zone defense that many modern teams have employed with great success, the 1-2-2 zone offense has been our offensive weapon against the "match-up" defense. The "match-up" defense will stymie the teams that use only movement and cutting methods to score against it. It is, however, vulnerable to the screening both on and away from the ball of the 1-2-2 zone offense.

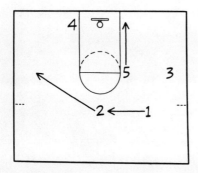

Diagram 70

ROTATION FROM THE FLIP-FLOP TO
THE 1-2-2 ZONE OFFENSE

The rotation from the Flip-Flop positions to the 1-2-2 is in a clockwise manner (Diagram 70).

After we are set up in the Flip-Flop positions, and call the 1-2-2, G^2 moves down to the wing; G^1 moves over and fills the point; high-post 5 drops down and sets up a double low post with low-post 4. We are now in the 1-2-2 alignment and are ready to run the offense.

THE FORWARD CLEAR OPTION

The forward clear option is another method of rotating from the Flip-Flop zone offense to the 1-2-2 zone offense, and a team can use this rotation to check their opponents' defenses. Many times defensive teams will stunt their defenses against an offense that uses their guards to determine the type of defense the opposition is using against them. Clearing a forward and sending him through the defense gives us still another method of determining the defense the opposition has set up against us.

This option is also a definite scoring threat to the defense as it offers good rotation and movement, as well as being an excellent method of checking the defense (Diagram 71).

Diagram 71 illustrates the forward clear option of the zone offense. This option is initiated from the Flip-Flop floor positions. G^1 clears F^3 out and through the defense; F^3 cuts through the defense and sets up on the opposite side of the floor at the wing position. G^1 passes to G^2 and slides down and fills F^3's vacated wing spot. Many times G^1 will be open for a jump shot by sliding down to the wing and catching the defensive man asleep in his area. If the defense does not follow F^3 through on his clear-out route, then the defense is in a zone defense. If, on the other hand, the defensive forward goes with him all the way through, then the defense is man-to-man. After F^3 has cleared through and set up on the opposite side of the floor and G^1 has filled F^3's original position, we

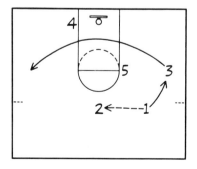

Diagram 71

interchange our pivot men, but this time their movement of interchange is straight up to the high post and down to the low post as
illustrated in Diagram 72. This interchange gives us good inside
movement and poses a scoring threat to the defense as low-post 4
looks for an opening in the defense while he rotates up and high-
post 5 also looks for an opening on his rotation to the baseline. This
inside rotation also offers us a secondary check of the defense that
our opponent is using against us.

THE BASELINE SCREEN OPTION

The baseline screen from the 1-2-2 offensive set has been one
of our most successful options against the zone defenses. We will
screen the zone initially on the baseline, looking for the short jump
shot. If we cannot get this shot, then we move the ball back to the
point and screen the zone from the weak side.

Diagram 73 illustrates the 1-2-2 alignment and movement of our
baseline screen option.

2 can initiate the baseline screen pattern by passing to either
3 or 1, who are the wing men. In this illustration, he passes to wing
man 3; 4 faces the ball on the baseline, and 5 cuts across the baseline behind 4, using him as a stationary baseline screen; 3 passes
to 5 if he is open on the baseline for the short jump shot. In the
event that 5 shoots the ball, 4 rebounds the lane area, 5 follows his

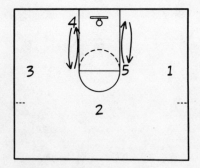

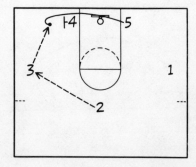

Diagram 72   *Diagram 73*

shot and rebounds the strong side of the board, and 1 is the weak-side rebounder.

After we have screened the baseline a few times and have shaken 5 open for the short jump shot, the defensive player guarding the baseline area where 4 is set up will anticipate 5's cut around 4 and will overcommit himself in order to cover 5. 3, upon seeing the defensive man widen out to cover 5, will pass inside to 4, who will have the defensive man that has come across to cover on his back and should be able to either score or draw a foul (Diagram 74).

If neither of these baseline screening options is successful, then we will move the ball back to the point and screen the ball from the weak side (Diagram 75A).

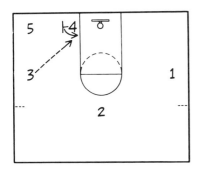

Diagram 74

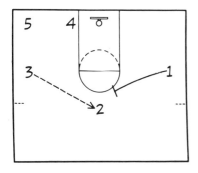

Diagram 75A

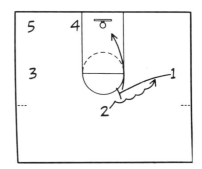

Diagram 75B

In the event that 4 is not open on the baseline, then we will look for secondary scoring opportunities from the baseline screen option. 3, upon seeing baseline men 4 and 5 not open, passes the ball quickly outside to point man 2. 1, who is the wing man on the weak side, comes up quickly and screens for 2, who dribbles over the top of the screen for a jump shot. If 2 takes the shot, 4 rebounds the lane area of the board, 5 is the weak-side rebounder, 1, who set the screen for 2, rolls to the strong side of the board to rebound (Diagram 75B).

NOTE: The zone defense must overshift toward the baseline screen in order to defend against it. This will enable our weak-side screen to be effective against this overshifting.

If point man 2 is unable to shoot the ball off weak-side wing man 1's screen, then he will flow into the third option of our 1-2-2 zone offense (Diagram 76). 2 has come over the top of 1's screen and is not open; 1 rolls to the basket; baseline men 5 and 4 close to set a double screen on the opposite baseline; wing man 3 moves out to receive a return pass from 2; 1 rolls to the basket and around the double screen set by 5 and 4; 3 feeds 1 behind the baseline double screen for the shot; 2 moves in and rebounds from opposite the double screen. If 1 takes the jump shot behind the double screen, then 2 is the weak-side rebounder, 5 rebounds the middle of the lane, and 4 is the strong-side rebounder. After his shot, 1 rotates outside to balance up.

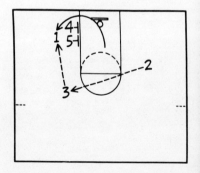

Diagram 76

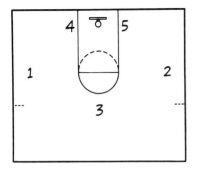

Diagram 77

If no shot is available, we will regroup from our 1-2-2 double screen baseline option with a rotation back into the 1-2-2 alignment. 5 moves across the lane and sets opposite 4 on the baseline, 3 is on the point, 1 and 2 fill the wing positions (Diagram 77).

The 1-2-2 zone offense, with a one-guard front and a double low post, is an excellent alignment from which to screen the zone defenses. The screening opportunities from the 1-2-2 offense, along with the constant movement we receive from the Flip-Flop zone offense, offer us an offensive combination capable of defeating any zone defense.

4

The Flip-Flop in
Ball Control Situations

Basketball games are consistently won by those teams that are able to protect their leads (point spreads) in the waning minutes of a close game with an effective ball control pattern. The question of when to begin ball control tactics has long been a nemesis to basketball coaches. There is no standard rule in determining when to go into a ball control type of pattern. The coach must consider such factors as tempo of the game, rhythm of the game, his team's ability to play a slow-down game, personnel, etc. It is important, however, that every coach have in his repertoire of offensive maneuvers a ball control pattern that will spread out the defense and eliminate possible double-team situations. It is important that a team be able to go into their ball control offense at any time during the course of a game with a minimum of adjustments.

The Flip-Flop ball control offense will afford the coach an excellent control type of pattern with a minimum of offensive regrouping. The Flip-Flop control pattern is built around the "basic three" of ball control movement. The "basic three" consist of: (1) offensive floor positioning in order to spread the defense out; (2) passing, cutting, and screening away from the ball in order to eliminate possible double-team situations; (3) maintaining offensive pressure on the defense in order to take advantage of defensive mistakes.

The success of any ball control pattern is highly dependent upon the discipline of the individual player in the tight pressure ball control situation. Discipline can only be developed by simulating ball control situations in daily practice. In setting up these actual game situations, the scoreboard and officials should be utilized, and, on occasion, the use of loud, artificial crowd noises will help condition the players to game situations. These ball control situations should vary daily in each daily practice session in order to expose the players to as many different situations as possible.

The floor positions in the Flip-Flop ball control offense are essentially the same as the basic man-to-man offense, with the exception of the offensive spacing. In ball control situations, we are attempting to spread the defense out, and in order to accomplish this, we must widen our offensive spacing.

Diagram 78 illustrates the floor positions for our ball control offense.

Guards G^1 and G^2 set up in the offensive guard area, three steps across the mid-court line. Strong-side forward F^3 sets up one step toward the baseline side of the foul lane extended and comes out high to receive any pass to him. High-post 4 sets up two steps up from the free-throw line extended and on the side of the key. This position is important because we want the lane area of the floor open for possible drives down the middle. Low-post man 5's posi-

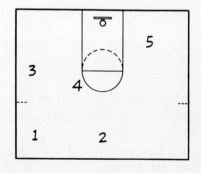

Diagram 78

tion is a wide forward position where he can receive a pass to start the pattern movement. He will, however, start from a low position and break out to receive the pass. His position and movement is the key to our ball control movement as we initiate our pattern from the weak side of the floor, going away from the high-post man and the congested side of the floor. Whenever we go into our Flip-Flop ball control offense, unlike the basic Flip-Flop Offense, we will, in certain options, rotate low-post 4 out to the perimeter of the offensive movement. In the "step out" option of our ball control offense, we will rotate both low-post 5 and high-post 4 outside.

Diagram 79 illustrates the basic movement of our ball control offense. First, in most instances, the guards will employ the guard hook-back maneuver discussed in Chapter 2 as a release against pressure. Notice that G^2 is executing the guard hook-back, thus clearing out the weak side of the floor enabling G^1 to come on the dribble and free low-post 5, who has stepped out to meet the pass and to start the offensive movement.

G^1, after his pass to low-post 5, executes a delayed cut down the middle looking for a return pass on a give-and-go maneuver. Many times, when encountering tight defensive pressure, G^1 will be open for a return pass on a quick cut to the basket (Diagram 80).

If G^1 is not open on his cut to the goal, then he circles out and replaces 5 at the low-post position. High-post 4, upon seeing that

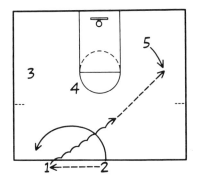

Diagram 79

G^1 is not open on his cut to the basket, moves across the lane and sets up at a high-post position. High-post 4 is the "safety valve" if low-post 5 gets into trouble from pressure.

Low-post 5, after looking for G^1 on his quick cut to the basket, dribbles out and fills the strong-side guard position. NOTE: High-post man 4 holds his position until low-post 5 puts the ball on the floor and starts to dribble out to the guard-side position. When low-post 5 starts his dribble, high-post man 4 moves across the lane and sets up a high-post position. At the same time, G^2 goes inside and sets a screen on F^3's man. It is important that G^2 hunt F^3's defensive man and set a positive screen on him (Diagram 81).

After he dribbles out to the guard position, 5 looks for F^3 who has come outside off of G^2's screen. If F^3 is open, he passes the ball to him and starts the pattern over on the opposite side of the floor with a pass to G^2 and a cut to the basket.

THE INTERCHANGE OPTION

In some instances, F^3 will not be open after G^2's screen. In these situations, 5 calls for help and high-post 4 comes high to the top of the key for a pass. 5 passes the ball to high-post 4 at this position,

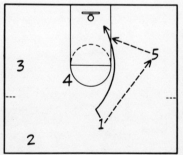

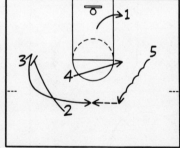

Diagram 80   Diagram 81

and then 3 and 5 go inside and set screens for 1 and 2. 4 can feed either 1 or 2, depending upon who is open first, and then assume his original position on the side of the lane (Diagram 82).

NOTE: Again, it is important that both 3 and 5 hunt the defensive men guarding 1 and 2 and set positive screens on them. 1 and 2 should line their men up for the screens by taking their defensive men inside a couple of steps before breaking out.

Diagram 83 illustrates the turnover after the pass to the high-post option.

THE BACK-DOOR OPTION

The back-door option is one of the most successful offensive weapons of the Flip-Flop ball control offense. The defenses we encounter whenever we employ our ball control offense are usually the pressure overplay type, and the back-door move is an excellent countermove against this type of defense.

We will set the back-door option up on the strong side after the high-post man has moved across the lane following the flow of the ball. The defensive forward is isolated in a one-on-one situation and can no longer rely on the defensive high-post man for help.

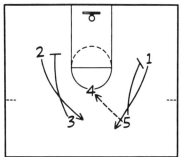

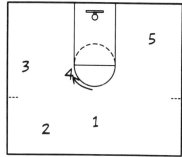

Diagram 82   *Diagram 83*

Diagram 84 illustrates the basic ball control pattern. 2 has passed to 5 and cut inside; 1 has gone inside to screen for 3 who is coming out to fill his vacated guard position; 5 has started his dribble outside to fill the vacated guard spot; and 4 is moving across the lane following the flow of the ball.

Diagram 85A illustrates the turnover of the basic pattern and the back-door option. 1 is now set up as the weak-side forward and is the one for whom we look on the back-door option. 5 has dribbled

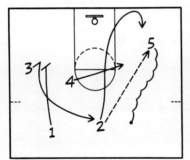 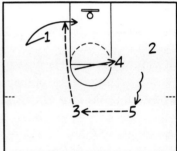

Diagram 84   Diagram 85A

out and passes to 3, 3 looks to feed 4 if he gets into trouble from defensive pressure, 1 comes high looking to receive a pass, and if his defensive man overcommits himself, he executes a quick back-door cut.

NOTE: High-post man 4 has moved across the lane taking his defensive man with him, thus taking a possible "sag" man away from the ball.

It is important that this back-door cut by the weak-side man be practiced daily and executed perfectly. We teach the player at the weak-side forward position to come out high to receive the pass and push off with the front foot when beginning his back-door cut to the basket.

In turning the basic pattern of the ball control offense over, we have rotated our forwards outside to the guard positions and we have rotated our guards inside to the forward positions. This inside and outside rotation of the players helps to set up the back-door option. The rotation of the forwards outside helps to relieve the defensive pressure and resistance we usually meet on the perimeter of the defense by the defensive guards. The rotation of the guards inside to the forward position enables us to take the defensive guards inside and force them to play defense at a forward position, a floor area where they are unaccustomed to playing defense.

NOTE: Most teams never drill and prepare their guards for playing defense inside on a forward or a post man.

The defensive guard, whenever defending from the (weak-side) forward position, is isolated in a one-on-one situation with no sagging or floating defensive help from his teammates. We have found our back-door option to be far more effective whenever our guards are rotated into the weak-side forward position.

The feeder (3) in executing the back-door option should make an exaggerated fake to feed the player at the weak-side forward position high and outside. This exaggerated fake by the feeder (3) will help to lure the inside defender higher out on the floor in an attempt to intercept the pass. This sets up the back-door cut to the basket. We have found that a bounce pass is the most effective pass to feed a player on this back-door cut. The bounce pass is the easiest to get by the defensive man who is guarding the passer and the easiest for the back-door cutter to handle.

The timing on the back-door option between the feeder and the cutter is the key to the success of the back-door option. This timing can only be developed and polished through constant repetition and drilling in the daily practice sessions.

Diagrams 85B and 85C illustrate our alternate back-door option to which we go whenever our opponent overplays and pressures our guard-to-guard pass on the perimeter of the floor.

Diagram 85B illustrates the basic back-door pattern and the rotation of the players. 2 passes inside to 5 and cuts down the lane, 5 after receiving the pass from 2 dribbles out to the perimeter of

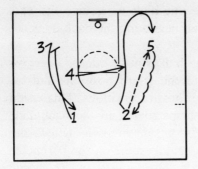

Diagram 85B

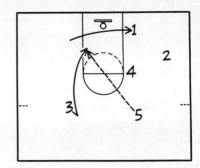

Diagram 85C

the floor. 4 moves across the lane following the flow of the ball and sets up a side post on the side of the lane.

Diagram 85C illustrates this variation from our basic back-door pattern.

You will notice that 1, after interchanging and screening for 3, has not set up on that side of the floor—he has cleared out across the lane. 5 dribbles out to the perimeter of the floor and fakes a pass to 3; if 3's defensive man overcommits himself, then 4 feeds 3 a bounce pass on a back-door cut.

In clearing across the lane, 1 has opened up the area underneath the goal for 3's back-door cut.

Many of our opponents, after we have scored on them several times with our basic back-door pattern, will adjust their defenses. They will in most instances cease to overplay the pass to the weak-side forward and instead overplay and pressure the guard-to-guard pass. Whenever this situation develops we will utilize this alternate back-door pattern.

NOTE: In the event that 3 is not open on his back-door cut, then 1 comes back across the lane to balance up the floor positions and we continue the basic pattern.

We key this option with a verbal signal. The verbal signal is given by the player (5), who is dribbling outside looking to pass to the player (3) coming off the interchange. The verbal signal we use is the word "red," which denotes danger. We feel that the guard-to-guard pass which the dribbler must execute is the most dangerous pass in basketball. If this perimeter pass is intercepted, it will result in a lay-up for our opponents. The success of this back-door option will depend a great deal upon player (1) reacting to the verbal signal and quickly clearing out across the lane.

THE STEP-OUT OPTION

The step-out is an option we have incorporated into our Flip-Flop ball control offense to open up the lane area and force the defensive pivot man outside into an unfamiliar defensive area. The step-out is the only option in our ball control offense that rotates all five players. In this option, we flex out from our original Flip-Flop alignment into the 3-2 alignment.

The step-out option can be utilized by the high-post man on any pass to him at the top of the key and in any "help" situation by a guard and an interchange between the guards and forwards. Whenever our guards are encountering difficulty out front from defensive pressure, we refer to this as a "help" situation (Diagram 86).

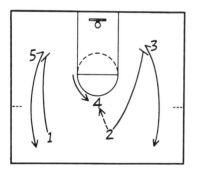

Diagram 86

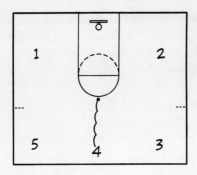

Diagram 87

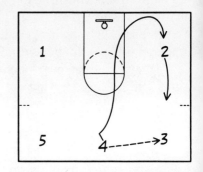

Diagram 88

The high-post man, upon receiving a pass at the top of the key, calls "step-out" and dribbles out to the middle of the floor. Upon seeing high-post 4 in the "step-out" option, 5 and 3, as they come off of the screens by the guards, flair out to the side of 4 and set up in a 3-2 alignment (Diagram 87).

NOTE: 1 and 2 set up inside and establish wide pivot positions.

From this 3-2 alignment, we go into a five-man rotation pattern with each player filling all five floor positions. The "step-out" pattern offers us several offensive opportunities, such as a give-and-go down the middle, the back-door cut, and the quickie cut.

Diagram 88 illustrates the basic "step-out" pattern. 4 has the option of passing to either 5, who has set up on one wing, or 3 on the other.

NOTE: It is important that the wing men take their defensive men in a couple of steps before coming out to receive a pass from 4. 4 passes to 3 and makes a quick cut to the basket looking for a return pass from 3 on a give-and-go maneuver. 4, if he does not receive a return pass, flows back to the side of the floor from which he made the pass and fills 2's inside position as 2 rotates outside. This movement has opened up the middle of the floor and offers the offense excellent opportunities for drives down the middle of the lane area. 3 now comes on the dribble looking for the easy drive down the middle area.

Diagram 89 illustrates the drive down the middle by 3 and the rotation of the offensive players.

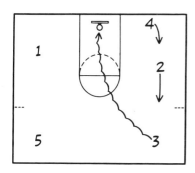

Diagram 89

NOTE: In our ball control offense we will, the majority of the time, instruct 3 to take this drive down the middle if he has it and if he can stay under control on his drive.

If 3 is unable to drive down the middle under control, he continues across the middle of the floor, passes the ball to 5, and executes a sharp cut down the lane looking for a return pass from 5 on a give-and-go maneuver (Diagram 90).

The basic step-out pattern can continue with 5 dribbling across and passing to 2 and cutting down the middle, etc. After we have turned this basic pattern over a couple of times and have rotated the defensive personnel both inside and outside, we look for the back-door option in the step-out pattern.

4 has passed to 3 and cuts sharply down the lane; 3 starts to dribble across the middle area and looks inside to 1, who is a wide pivot man and has broken up to the edge of the key for a pass from 3. 3 feeds inside to 1; 5 holds his position as 3 makes the pass inside to 1; 5's defensive man, in many instances, will turn his head to locate the position of the ball, and if he does, 5 immediately executes a back-door cut and 1 feeds him a bounce pass for the lay-up (Diagram 91).

NOTE: The pass from 1 to 5 on the back-door cut should be a bounce pass, as this is the easiest type of pass for 1 to get by the inside defensive man guarding him. His defensive man will be playing him with arms extended high, so we instruct him to feed the ball low and away from his defensive man by using the bounce pass. This back-door cut in our step-out pattern is one of our most effective moves in a ball control situation. Many times we have scored two or three consecutive baskets in tight pressure situations.

THE "QUICKIE" OPTION

The "quickie" is another option in our step-out pattern that we use as a countermove against teams that overplay us both outside and inside on our step-out pattern. The "quickie" forces the defense to make quick adjustments with both their perimeter defense and their interior defense. We have found that by utilizing the "quickie" option against tight defensive overplay, it has helped to keep the defense honest and has been an excellent release against the tight defensive overplay.

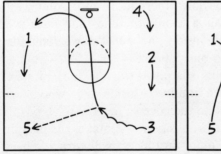

Diagram 90

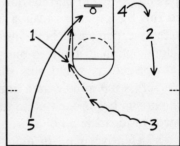

Diagram 91

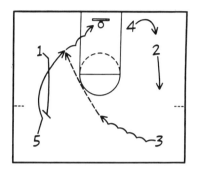

Diagram 92

Diagram 92 illustrates our "quickie" option. 4 has executed the step-out; he has passed to 3 and cut to the basket. 3 has started his dribble across the floor; wing man 5 and wide pivot man 1 are encountering high pressure overplays by their defensive men. 1 must key the "quickie" upon seeing the defensive pivot man playing him high on his overplay, and seeing 5's defensive man overplaying him high, he steps up quickly and sets a back block for 5, opening up a back side cut. 3 passes to 5 after his back side cut for a lay-up.

NOTE: Wing man 5 would be taking his defensive man inside two or three steps against an overplay, thus lining him up for the back block by 1.

If 5 is not open on his cut to the basket, or 3 is unable to feed him, 1 steps out and fills 5's vacated wing position; 5, after his cut, fills 1's vacated wide pivot position. We have now performed an interchange between 5 and 1 and can continue the basic pattern with 3 feeding 5 and cutting to the basket (Diagram 93, next page).

NOTE: In stepping out after setting his back block for 5, 1 will be open in the event the defense switches, and can continue the pattern.

THE CIRCLE ROTATION OPTION

The circle rotation option is an offensive maneuver we employ whenever we become static in our offensive movement. In many instances, our ball control offense will encounter defenses that will clog up our offensive cutting routes and effectively anticipate almost

every move of our basic pattern. Whenever this happens, our circle
rotation option, which rotates the defensive men to different posi-

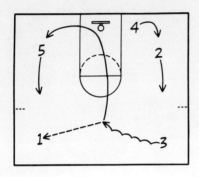

Diagram 93

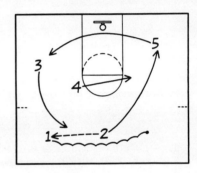

Diagram 94

tions, gives us the variation from the basic pattern we need to keep
the defense off balance.

Diagram 94 illustrates the circle rotation option. 2 has the ball
and is unable to feed 5 to start our basic ball control pattern. 2
passes to 1 and fills 5's position; 1 dribbles over and fills 2's vacated
guard position. 3 rotates out to 1's vacated position, and 5 comes
across and fills 3's vacated forward position; high-post man 4 moves
across the lane and sets up a high-post position.

NOTE: 3 can initiate the ball control offense by passing to 5 and
cutting to the basket. 5 will be able to free himself from an overplay
with this quick change to the opposite side of the floor.

Diagram 95 illustrates the turnover of the circle rotation option.
We are now ready to run any of the other options of our ball control
offense.

We key our circle rotation pattern verbally by calling "circle" and
rotating into it. We feel this rotation pattern has given us the varia-

tion in our movement which we have needed against the strong defensive ball clubs that contain our basic pattern.

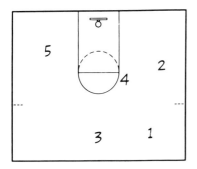

Diagram 95

5

The Flip-Flop and
Special Situations

Basketball coaches today are spending more and more time preparing for special situations that they will encounter during the course of a basketball game. These special situations will include out-of-bounds plays, jump balls, last second shot situations, etc. The team that is well disciplined and prepared to handle these special situations when they occur will have the poise and confidence to win the close games that makes for a successful season.

In each of our daily practice sessions, we allot 10 to 15 minutes to instructions on special situations. We try to vary these situations in order to cover as many different ones as possible during this practice time.

Coach Ken Trickey, former head basketball coach at Middle Tennessee State University, has contributed some of the special situation patterns and maneuvers that we will discuss in this chapter.

In preparing to encounter these special situations, we coordinate the Flip-Flop with these situations whenever possible. In our coordination of the Flip-Flop and special situations, we set up a special situation play or pattern and upon completion of this play or pattern, if we have not scored, then we are set up in the Flip-Flop alignment. We are then ready to run our pattern offense rather than having to regroup and delay our offensive attack.

We are now going to discuss some of the special situation plays we have utilized during past seasons. Again, the coach's theory and philosophy concerning these special situations will vary from season to season depending upon his team personnel, strength of opposition, etc.

The diagrams which follow illustrate some of the special situation alignments and patterns that we have utilized during past seasons.

OUT-OF-BOUNDS SITUATIONS

The out-of-bounds situations that develop during the course of a basketball game will present excellent scoring opportunities to a team. A team in possession of the basketball out of bounds in their offensive end of the court should be prepared to attack any defense that they might encounter.

There are two schools of thought concerning the theory of offensing out-of-bounds situations. The first of the two theories advocates that a team gear the out-of-bounds patterns simply to getting the ball into play in their offensive end of the court and then setting up their regular offense. The logic behind this type of out-of-bounds pattern is that a team's regular offense is better prepared to attack the defense than an out-of-bounds pattern. Also, the extra practice time spent on intricate out-of-bounds patterns could be better utilized in preparation for the regular offense.

The second school of thought concerning the offensive out-of-bounds situation is a team employing a planned pattern of attack whose purpose and goal is to score. I, personally, advocate the planned pattern of attack designed to score for offensive out-of-bounds situations. I have seen many close basketball games won in the closing seconds with a planned pattern of attack from an out-of-bounds situation.

UNDER THE BASKET PATTERNS

Whenever we are awarded the ball out of bounds underneath our basket, we will set up in one of two different offensive alignments. These two alignments are known as the "Box" alignment and the "Three Horsemen" alignment.

The Box Alignment

The first of the under the basket alignments we shall discuss is the "Box" alignment. The Box alignment is probably the most popular and most widely used out-of-bounds formation in the game of basketball today.

Diagram 96 illustrates the first option from the Box alignment that we employ against a man-to-man defense.

G^1 sets up out of bounds to signal the option we will run from this alignment and to pass the ball in from out of bounds. High-post man 5 and weak-side forward 4 set up underneath the basket on

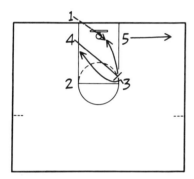

Diagram 96

each side of the foul lane. Weak-side guard 2 and strong-side forward 3 set up on each side of the foul lane extended. The floor position of the four in-bounds players forms a box formation.

G^1 puts the pattern in motion by slapping the ball, 5 breaks out to the opposite corner yelling for G^1 to pass the ball to him, 4 breaks up to the foul lane extended and sets a screen on 3, 3 breaks over the top of 4's screen and cuts straight into 4's vacated position. 4 in screening for 3 holds his screen on 3 long enough to invite the defense to switch, 4 then pivots and rolls underneath the basket for a pass from 1. 4, if he is open, will receive the pass from 1 in the open floor area that 5 has vacated by going to the corner and taking his defensive man with him.

NOTE: 5 in clearing out of the area underneath the basket by going to the corner should always yell to 1 for the pass and force his defensive man to follow him. If 3 is wide open coming off of 4's screen, then 1 should be instructed to pass to him. In the event that the defense switches on 4's screen, then 4 will have a defensive man on his back on his roll to the basket. This is a very effective out-of-bounds pattern against a team that switches on all screening situations.

Diagram 97 illustrates how we rotate into our Flip-Flop floor positions from the Box alignment in the event the out-of-bounds pattern is not successful.

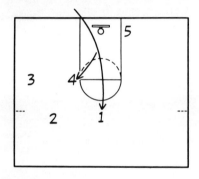

Diagram 97

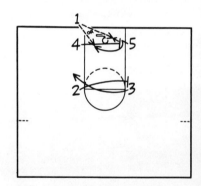

Diagram 98

The rotation is as follows: 3, after his cut-off of 4's screen, sets up at the strong-side forward position, 2 widens out the strong-side guard position, 4 cuts up the lane and sets up at the high-post position, 5 moves in from the corner and sets up at the weak-side forward position, and 1 moves up the lane from out of bounds and fills the weak-side guard position. We are now set up in the Flip-Flop alignment and are ready to attack the defense.

The second option from the Box alignment is a simple screening maneuver that we also utilize against teams that defense screening situations by switching (Diagram 98).

4 moves across the lane and sets a screen on 5's defensive man, 5 fakes to the baseline and comes over the top of 4's screen. In some instances when the defense does not switch, 5 will be open for a high pass directly underneath the basket. However, 4 is the primary receiver in this pattern. After setting his screen on 5's defensive man, he holds his screen until 5 has cut by him. After 5 has cut by the screen, 4 pivots, takes one step to the basket, and if the defense has switched he will have the defensive man on his back. 2 and 3 simply interchange with 2 moving over and setting a screen on 3's defensive man. 3 comes over the top of the screen and moves out wide to receive a pass from 1. 3 serves as the "safety valve" in most cases for this pattern in that he will receive the ball from 1 only if 4 and 5 are not open.

NOTE: It is important that 4, in setting his screen on 5, hunt 5's defensive man down and execute a positive screen on him. Also it is important that 4 hold his screen until his defensive man has had the opportunity to switch off and take 5 coming across. This option has given us many three point plays underneath the basket. Whenever an offensive post man gets the ball underneath the basket with his defensive man on his back he is almost impossible to defense.

Diagram 99 illustrates the rotation from this pattern into the Flip-Flop positions.

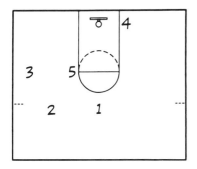

Diagram 99

3 sets up at the strong-side forward, 5 moves up the lane and sets up at the high-post position, 4 sets up at the weak-side forward position, 2 moves out and sets up at the strong-side guard position, 1 comes out and fills the weak-side guard position.

The third option from the Box alignment is an excellent pattern by which to set up scoring opportunities against a team that will switch defensively on all screening situations.

Diagram 100 illustrates the third option from the Box alignment.

1 signals the pattern from out of bounds, 3 executes the first movement in the pattern. 3 clears across the lane and sets up a double screen with 4 at the side of the foul lane. 5 times his movement and holds until 3 is about halfway through on his clear-out route. 5 then breaks up to the foul lane extended and sets a back-block on 2's defensive man. 2 then cuts over the top of 5's screen and under the goal for a pass from 1 and a basket. Against teams that refuse to switch against positive screens this is an effective option to run.

After this pattern has been run successfully several times, teams will usually adjust defensively and will set their defenses to switch on 5's back-block. Against teams that adjust defensively to the third option by switching on 5's back-block we will run the counter-option off of the pattern.

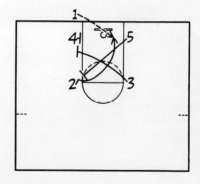

Diagram 100

Diagram 101 illustrates the counter-option that we run against teams that switch defensively on 5's back-block.

4 and 5 have formed a double screen at the side of the foul lane, 5 has set the back-block on 2, 2 has cut over the top of the back-block and under the goal. In the event 5's defensive man switches off and picks up 2 coming over the top of the back-block on his cut to the basket, then 5 rolls down behind 4 and 3's double screen at the side of the lane. 1 passes to 5 behind the double screen for a short-range jump shot.

Diagram 102 illustrates the organized rotation from the third option of the Box alignment into the Flip-Flop positions.

3 flares out and sets up at the strong-side forward position, 4 moves across the lane and establishes a weak-side forward position, 2 sets up at a strong-side guard position, 5 moves up to the high-post position, and 1 comes from out of bounds to the outside and sets up at the weak-side guard position.

The fourth option from the Box alignment is a zone offense pattern that is designed to counterattack any team that elects to set up a zone defense against out-of-bounds patterns. Many of the coaches of today subscribe to the theory of zoning all defensive out-of-bounds situations. The 2-3 zone is the type of zone that is employed most often.

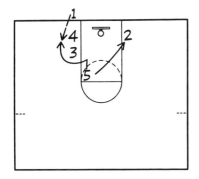

Diagram 101

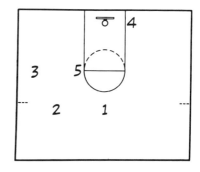

Diagram 102

Diagram 103 illustrates the fourth option of the Box alignment designed to offense the zone defense.

1 signals the pattern from out of bounds, 2 breaks out to the corner for a pass from 1, 4 moves up the lane to the high post, 1 passes to 2 in the corner, 2 passes to 3 who has broken out to the top of the key. 1, who has passed the ball in from out of bounds, breaks to the opposite side of the floor and cuts around a screen set by 5. 3 passes the ball to 1, who takes a medium-range jump shot behind 5's screen.

The effectiveness of this pattern is due mainly to the fact that 1 puts the ball into play on the strong side of the floor, then breaks to the weak side of the floor for the shot. This offensive maneuver will force the zone to overshift to the strong side of the floor to defense 1's in-bounds pass to 2, then react back to the weak side of the floor. In most cases, the zone will not be able to recover defensively in time to defend against 1's jump shot on the weak side of the floor.

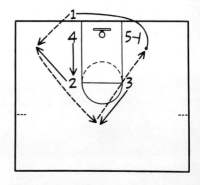

Diagram 103

The Three Horsemen Alignment

The second offensive formation we will utilize in under the basket situations is the "Three Horsemen" alignment. The term "Three Horsemen" was derived from the positioning of three offensive players side by side at the free-throw line.

Several summers ago while attending a coaching clinic with a good friend of mine, Fran Florient, former Georgia Southern basketball great, Fran showed me this out-of-bounds pattern. This pattern has proved to be almost impossible to stop since we installed it against man-to-man defenses.

Diagram 104 illustrates the Three Horsemen alignment and the first option for under the basket out-of-bounds situations against man-to-man defenses.

The player positions for this pattern are as follows: 1 is stationed out of bounds where he signals the pattern and makes the in-bounds pass; 3, 4 and 5 line up side by side at the free-throw line; 2 sets up underneath the basket on the opposite side of the foul lane from 1. We usually station our best jump shooter at the 2 position.

1 signals the option and slaps the ball to put the pattern in motion. 4 and 5 move down the lane together at a right angle, away from the ball, forming a double screen for 3 to rub his defensive man off on his cut. 3 takes one step down the lane and comes back

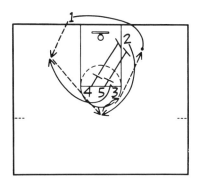

Diagram 104

over the top of the double screen set by 4 and 5; he then cuts across the court to the side of the court. 1 passes to 3 who is open on the side of the court. 4 and 5, who initially set the double screen for 3, continue on down the lane together forming a double screen for 2 to rub his defensive man off on while coming over the top of the screen to the top of the key. 3 after receiving the pass from 1 looks immediately for 2 coming to the top of the key. If he is open 3 passes to 2 for a short jump shot. In most instances, either 3 or 2 on the side or at the top of the key will be successful in rubbing their defensive man off and will be open for a jump shot. In the event that either 3 or 2 are unable to score or take a shot, they will look for 1. 1 will break from out of bounds to the opposite side of the floor and cut behind a double screen set at the side of the foul lane by 4 and 5. 2 will take a couple of dribbles in order to improve his passing angle to 1 and feeds him behind the double screen for a jump shot.

NOTE: 4 and 5, after first setting moving double screens for 3 and 2 respectively, station themselves at the side of the foul lane forming a double screen for 1.

This is an intricate pattern with a lot of offensive movement. The timing between the players on their cuts and screens cannot be overemphasized in teaching this particular option.

Diagram 105 illustrates the rotation from the first option of the Three Horsemen alignment into the Flip-Flop positions.

3 sets up at the strong-side forward, 5 moves up and establishes a high-post position, 4 sets up at a weak-side forward position, 2 moves over to the strong-side guard position, 1 sets up at a weak-side guard position.

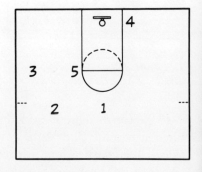

Diagram 105

After we have run the first option several times, the defense usually attempts to stop the pattern by switching off on 3 and attempting to stop the initial in-bounds pass to 3 on the side of the court. Whenever the defense switches or overplays 3 as we have explained, then we automatically set up the second option as a countermove to this defensive stunt.

Diagram 106 illustrates the second option of the Three Horsemen alignment.

This particular option is designed to set up scoring opportunities on the opposite side of the floor from the first option. 1 signals the pattern from out of bounds, and 2 clears across the lane and sets up at the side of the lane. In this option 5 and 3 form the double screen and 4 is the first cutter. 4 takes a step down the lane, then he cuts around the double screen and underneath the basket to the area cleared out by 2. 1 passes to 4 underneath the basket for an easy score. 5 and 3 after setting their double screen for 4 continue on down the lane and form a double screen for 2 to rub his defensive man off on while cutting to the top of the key. If 4 cannot score or shoot the ball, he will look for 2 at the top of the key for a jump shot.

In positioning your personnel in this pattern, it would be wise to station your best shooter at the 2 position.

Diagram 107 illustrates the rotation from the second option of

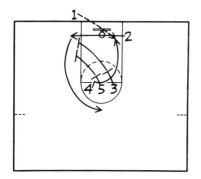

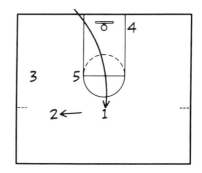

Diagram 106   *Diagram 107*

the Three Horsemen alignment into the Flip-Flop positions.

3 establishes a strong-side forward position, 5 moves up to the high-post position, 4 sets up at the weak-side forward position, 2 moves over to the strong-side guard position, and 1 sets up at the weak-side guard position.

Side Out-of-Bounds

Whenever a team is rewarded the ball on a side out-of-bounds situation, it presents them with the opportunity to attack the defense from a different angle and with a variation from their basic offensive pattern. Many teams in their defensive preparations will allot all of their practice time to defense a team's basic pattern, and will not be prepared defensively against special situations.

Our philosophy concerning side out-of-bounds situations is the same as with under the basket situations. We are attempting to score from these situations whenever possible.

Diagram 108 illustrates the first of our side out-of-bounds scoring patterns.

1 from the side out-of-bounds position signals the pattern. High-post man 4 rolls down the lane and screens the defensive man guarding 5; 5 takes two steps to the baseline in order to line his defensive men up for 4's screen, then 5 cuts over the top of 4's screen to the high-post area; 1 passes to 5 at the high-post area; 3 moves up quickly and sets a back-block on the defensive player

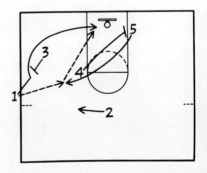

Diagram 108

guarding 1 out of bounds; 1 executes a quick cut to the basket via the back-door route utilizing 3's screen on his defensive man; 5 passes to 1 for the lay-up. In most instances, 5's pass to 1 should be a bounce pass because this type of pass will be the easiest to get by his own defensive man.

The success of this side out-of-bounds pattern will be due mainly to the fact that most teams in defending against such situations tend to disregard the player handling the ball out of bounds. On many occasions, after the in-bounds pass has been made, the defensive player guarding the offensive player out of bounds will then turn his head. This carelessness on the part of the defensive player should be taken advantage of whenever possible during the course of a game.

Diagram 109 illustrates the rotation from this side out-of-bounds pattern into the Flip-Flop positions.

2 moves over and fills the strong-side guard position; 3, after setting his screen for 1, fills the strong-side forward position; 5 sets up at the high-post position; and 4 sets up at the weak-side forward position. 1, after his back-door cut, circles outside and sets up at the weak-side guard position.

Diagram 110 illustrates the second of our side out-of-bounds patterns.

In this particular pattern, 4 and 5 set up together on the opposite side of the floor at the side of the foul lane. 1 signals the pattern from his out-of-bounds position; 5 executes the first movement of the pattern by cutting directly down the lane. 5 should execute

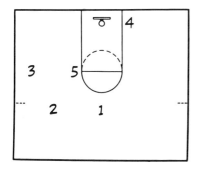

Diagram 109

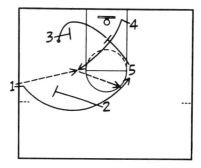

Diagram 110

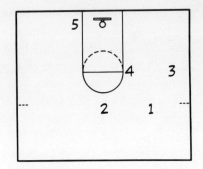

Diagram 111

his cut at such an angle that 4 can rub his defensive man off on him; 4 times his move so as to rub his defensive man off on 5 as 5 cuts down the lane; 4 cuts over the top of 5 to the high-post area. 3 goes low to the baseline and sets a screen for 5. 5, after his cut down the lane, comes around the screen set by 3 looking for a pass from 1 and a possible jump shot. 1 has the alternative of either passing to 4 or 5. In either case, after 1 passes the ball in-bounds, 2 moves across to screen 1's defensive man. 1 cuts around 2's screen to the opposite side of the court looking for a return pass from either 4 or 5. You will notice we have flooded the strong side of the court with all five offensive players.

After flooding the strong side, 1 will then cut from out of bounds back to the weak side of the court. 1 will, in most instances, have a wide open jump shot or an excellent one-on-one situation with the weak-side area of the court cleared out for him to operate in.

NOTE: Unlike our first side out-of-bounds pattern, where 1 executed a baseline cut to the basket from his out-of-bounds position, 1 cuts to the weak side of the floor via the outside route. This maneuver makes it almost impossible for the defender guarding 1 out of bounds to play 1 to either side of the court on every out-of-bounds situation.

This pattern would be excellent for the team with a "super star" whom they attempt to set up whenever possible. They could station him at the 1 position out of bounds and then break him to the cleared-out weak side of the floor.

Diagram 111 illustrates the rotation from this side out-of-bounds pattern into the Flip-Flop positions.

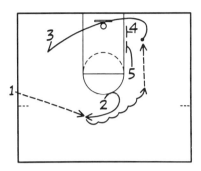

Diagram 112

3 moves across the court after setting his screen for 5 and sets up at the strong-side forward position. 4 moves over and sets up at the high-post position. 1 fills the strong-side guard position. 2 fills the weak-side guard position. 5 is already at the weak-side forward position and remains there.

Diagram 112 illustrates the third of our side out-of-bounds patterns.

Again we set 4 and 5 up together at the side of the foul lane on the opposite side of the floor. 1 signals the pattern from his position out of bounds. 2 takes one step away from the ball, then moves to meet the ball. 1 passes to 2, and 4 and 5 close up the distance between them to form a double screen (the double screen formed by 4 and 5 should be set as close to the baseline as possible).

2, after receiving the in-bounds pass, dribbles toward the double screen formed by 4 and 5. 2 passes to 3 for a short jump shot behind the double screen. We have gone to this pattern whenever teams we faced would sag or float their defensive players guarding 4 and 5 in the lane area. This defensive sagging and floating would make it almost impossible for either 4 or 5 to free themselves by moving to meet the ball. However, by utilizing 4 and 5 as a double screen on the weak side of the floor, we have inactivated 4 and 5's defensive men who are sagging in the lane. They will not be able to switch off and help out on 3 behind the double screen because their defensive sag has carried them too far away from the double screen.

NOTE: You will also notice that the in-bounds pass in this pattern was made to the outside to 2. In the other patterns, the in-bounds pass was made inside to either 5 or 4. This pattern will also serve as a countermove against any team that attempts to stunt their defense to cut off our passing inside on them.

Diagram 113 illustrates our rotation from this side out-of-bounds pattern into the Flip-Flop positions.

3 moves out from behind the double screen and sets up at the strong-side forward position. 5 moves up to the high-post position. 4 moves across the lane and establishes a weak-side forward position. 2 sets up at a strong-side guard position, and 1 fills the weak-side guard position.

LAST SECOND SHOT SITUATIONS

Remember that the key to a successful season for a basketball team is the ability to win the close ball games. In the course of a basketball season, many games are won or lost in the waning seconds of the game. A team should always include in its offensive preparations a planned last second scoring pattern. This pattern, or patterns, should be simulated under pressure type conditions whenever possible in the daily practice sessions.

The last second scoring pattern of a team will often vary from year to year depending upon who is the best shooter, pressure player, one-on-one player, etc. This personnel change from year to year will dictate in many cases whether or not a team's last

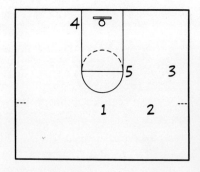

Diagram 113

second scoring opportunity will be a one-on-one situation, a jump shot situation, a driving situation, etc.

The diagrams which follow illustrate a few of the last second scoring patterns we have utilized during past seasons. You will notice we do not have an organized rotation from our last second shot patterns into the basic Flip-Flop positions. This is due mainly to the fact that since we are playing for a last second scoring attempt, time does not permit us to flow back into the basic pattern.

Diagram 114 illustrates a last second scoring pattern that will set up the high-post man for a short jump shot.

1 passes to 3 and cuts to the basket on a give-and-go maneuver. In the event that 1 does not receive a return pass, he sets up on the opposite side of the foul lane. 1 and 5 form a double screen at the side of the foul lane. 3 then passes back outside to 2; 4 rolls down the lane and cuts around the double screen formed by 1 and 5 at the side of the lane. 2 passes to 4 behind the double screen for a short-range jump shot. 2, after his pass to 4 behind the double screen, goes inside and sets a screen for 3; 3 comes over the top of the screen, and if 4 is unable to get behind the double screen, he looks for 3 coming over the top of 2's screen.

Diagram 115 illustrates a last second scoring pattern that will isolate a guard and a forward in a two-on-two situation. This pattern also contains a counter-option to combat a team's sagging or floating by the defense.

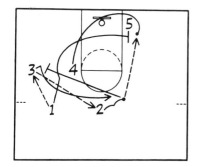

Diagram 114

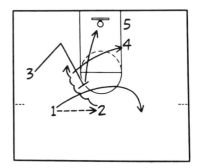

Diagram 115

1 passes to 2 and executes a "hook-back" maneuver; 4 clears out from the high-post position and moves across the lane, setting up beside 5. This movement has now isolated the forward (3) and the guard (2) on one side of the floor. 3 quickly moves up to the edge of the key and sets a screen on 2's defensive man. 2 comes over the top of the screen, looking for the jump shot or the drive; 3, after screening for 2, rolls to the basket. 3 will be open in the event of a switch by the defense.

This scoring pattern will be successful for the team that has a guard and a forward who are good offensive ball players and who work well together in a two-on-two situation. The screen and roll maneuver used in this pattern by the guard and forward is one of the finest offensive weapons in the game of basketball today.

Diagram 116 illustrates the countermove of the pattern to combat any sagging or floating by the defense.

2 and 3 work the two-on-two maneuver with 2 coming over the top of 3's screen. 2, upon seeing the defensive men guarding 5 and 4 sagging in the lane area, quickly pivots and passes out to 1. 5 steps out behind 4's screen for a quick pass from 1 and a short jump shot. 5's defensive man, who was sagging in the lane, will be unable to defend against 5's jump shot behind 4's screen. This quick movement of the ball back to the weak side of the floor will prevent the defense from sagging on the two-on-two play.

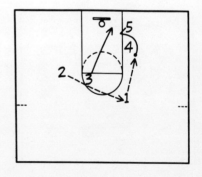

Diagram 116

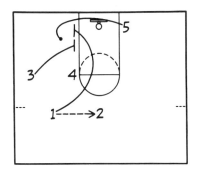

Diagram 117

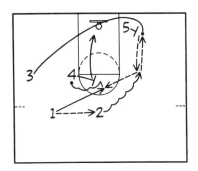

Diagram 118

Diagram 117 illustrates a last second scoring pattern that will set up a one-on-one situation for the guard and also will offer a triple screening situation to set up a jump shot on the weak side of the floor.

1 passes to 2 and cuts down the foul lane, setting up on the baseline at the side of the lane. 3 moves in and sets up at the side of the foul lane forming a triple screen with 4 and 1. 5 clears across the lane and cuts around behind the triple screen. This movement has succeeded in clearing out the side of the floor where 2 now has the ball in a one-on-one situation. 2 has the choice of driving his defensive man to the basket or taking the ball on the dribble and passing the ball to 5 behind the triple screen for a short-range jump shot.

For the team with a guard who is an outstanding offensive basketball player and who is almost impossible to stop in a one-on-one situation, this pattern will be made to order.

Diagram 118 illustrates a last second scoring pattern against a zone defense.

1 signals for 3 to clear out to the opposite side of the floor; 1 passes to 2; 3, after his clear-out, comes around 5 who is on the baseline; 5 screens the defensive man covering the area; 2 dribbles toward 3, and if 3 is open, 2 feeds him behind the baseline screen for a jump shot. In the event 3 is not able to take the shot, he

passes quickly back to 2; 2 passes to 1; 4 steps out and sets a screen on the defensive man guarding 1's area; 1 comes over the top of 4's screen for a jump shot. This quick movement of the ball back to the weak side of the floor for the jump shot will be successful against many of the zone defenses. The zone defense will be forced to over-shift in their coverage in order to defend against 3's jump shot behind 5's screen. If the zone does not overshift in its coverage of 3, then 3 should have no difficulty in freeing himself for a jump shot. In the event that the zone does overshift in its coverage, then the quick movement of the ball back to the weak side of the floor will succeed in freeing 1 for the jump shot.

Utilizing the "Huddle" During Free-Throw Situations

A basketball team is allotted five time-outs during a regulation basketball game. These time-outs are utilized by a team for the purpose of uniting all five players to discuss their offensive strategy, defensive strategy, and to reinforce team morale. These five allotted time-outs will not be sufficient to handle all of the different situations that a team will encounter during the course of a basketball game; therefore, a team should wisely take advantage of any opportunity to supplement these time-outs by bringing all five players together on the floor during a dead ball situation.

Coach Garland Pinholster, head basketball coach at Oglethorpe College and one of basketball's keenest tacticians, was one of the first basketball coaches to utilize a method of huddling his players on the floor during a dead ball situation. Coach Pinholster's assistant coach, John Guthrie, and Donnie Newman, a former player of mine while coaching at Martin College, used the huddle and convinced Coach Ken Trickey and me of the merits of this huddle maneuver. John felt that not only was the huddle maneuver of benefit to the Oglethorpe basketball staff in plotting their offensive and defensive strategy on the floor, but it was also a tremendous morale booster. Bringing together all five players on the floor helps to strengthen the esprit de corps of a ball club.

With this in mind, several seasons ago we installed the huddle at Middle Tennessee, using it exclusively during free-throw situations. We now instruct our players whenever a personal foul is assessed by an official to quickly form a huddle beside the foul lane where the free throw is to be administered. During this huddle our floor leader will give the players their offensive and defensive instructions.

If the personal foul is assessed against our opponents, then our floor leader will give the players their defensive instructions in the huddle. In the event the personal foul is assessed against our team, then the floor leader will issue to the players their offensive instructions. Since this book is concerned with our offensive procedures, we shall discuss only the offensive benefits of the huddle.

Diagram 119 illustrates the areas on the floor where the huddle is formed during the free-throw situations.

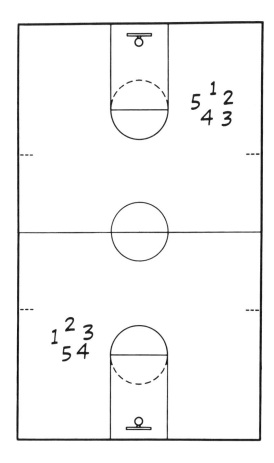

Diagram 119

The huddle will always be formed just beyond the top of the key area and on the right side of the floor. This particular area of the floor permits us to huddle without interfering with player traffic or, more important, interfering with the officials near the free-throw line. This area of the floor is located close enough to the free-throw line to enable us to huddle without delaying the free-throw process. Another important point is that the huddle maneuver is legal and will be acceptable to the officials as long as it is formed quickly and does not delay the free-throw process.

Our floor leader is always a guard, because he has the responsibility of penetrating the defense and initiating the offensive pattern. The offensive instructions our floor leader will issue will vary with the defensive situations we will encounter, game tempo, team personnel, etc. However, in general, the offensive instructions our players receive from the huddle are as follows: The Flip-Flop option we will run the next time down the floor, the alternative pattern we will go to in the event the first option is not successful. Whenever we are playing against an opponent that utilizes pressing defenses after successful free throws, our floor leader will alert the players in the huddle for the press. The alerting of our players in the huddle for the pressing defenses has been instrumental in our success against the presses. The huddle has taken away the surprise element of the pressing defense and has helped to eliminate the possibility that our players may push the panic button when encountering the pressing defenses.

When installing the huddle maneuver, there are several important teaching points that have helped to make the huddle so successful. First, the floor leader must always signal for the huddle immediately after the official calls a personal foul. This is emphasized in our daily practice sessions. Secondly, the huddle must be timed during both game and practice sessions. In our daily practice sessions the huddle is timed and a maximum of four seconds is allowed after the huddle has been formed. During these daily practice sessions, this timing of the huddle is rigidly enforced. Each time the huddle exceeds its time limit in a practice scrimmage the opposing team is awarded two points. This timing and enforcement in installing the huddle has helped to bring about the necessary speed in assembling and disassembling the huddle.

JUMP BALL SITUATIONS

In discussing jump ball situations and our theory concerning them, possession of the basketball is our main objective. Jump ball situations are unlike out-of-bounds situations in that a team already has possession of the basketball and is attempting to score; whereas, in the jump ball situation, neither team has possession of the basketball. In organizing our offensive planning concerning jump ball situations, we are attempting first to gain possession of the basketball, and second, to score.

There are many intricate jump ball maneuvers designed to shake a player loose for a quick score, but the jump ball situations that will arise during the course of a season will be too numerous for a team to depend upon these intricate maneuvers. On many occasions these intricate jump ball maneuvers will prove much too complicated as the opposing team gains possession of the basketball.

Simplicity is the key to our jump ball organization. A basketball player cannot be confused and at the same time aggressive. Simplicity and aggressiveness go hand in hand in our jump ball preparations as both are of the utmost importance. Our players react to the jump ball situations with the same aggressiveness as in the rebounding situations. We instruct those lined up around the perimeter of the circle who are to be receivers to utilize the jack-knife maneuver in receiving the basketball. The jack-knife maneuver is a technique we teach in our rebounding drills. This is an important teaching point in preparing a team for the jump ball situation, and it helps to add the aggressiveness so necessary in these situations.

We utilize two different alignments during the jump ball situations. The areas of the floor where the jump ball situation develops will dictate to us which of the two alignments we will utilize. The "Y" alignment will be utilized whenever the jump ball situation takes place at the mid-court area. The Box alignment will be utilized whenever the jump ball situation takes place at either foul lane area.

The first jump ball alignment we will discuss is the "Y" alignment, which we automatically set up whenever jump ball situations occur at the mid-court area.

The "Y" jump ball alignment as illustrated in Diagram 120 is formed with 5 setting up in the circle as the jumper. 4 and 3 set up in our offensive court on the perimeter of the circle. 4 and 3 are the primary receivers in the "Y" formation. 2 sets up in the back court on the perimeter of the circle. 1 sets up as the deep safety man in the back court and forms the tail of the "Y." This jump ball alignment at mid-court offers us excellent offensive possession opportunities, while at the same time giving us excellent defensive coverage. If our opponent decides to match up with us while we are

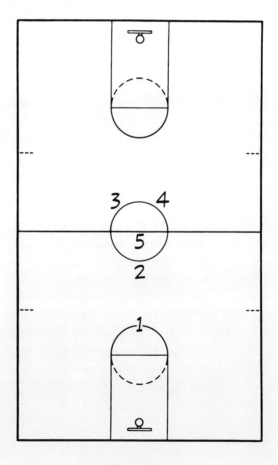

Diagram 120

in the "Y" jump ball alignment, then we will have offensive spacing. With this offensive spacing we have succeeded in isolating 4 and 3 in a two-on-two situation. If we are able to gain the tip, these two isolated offensive players should be able to maneuver to gain possession of the basketball. In the event that our opponent gains possession on the tip, then we are still able to maintain good defensive floor coverage with 2 and 1 defending the scoring area until their teammates can recover.

If our opponent elects not to match up with us in the "Y" align-

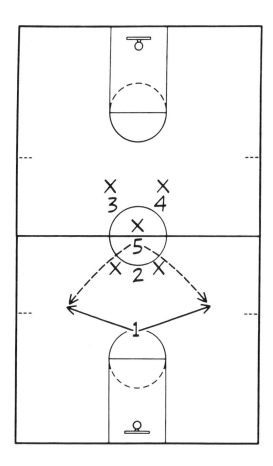

Diagram 121

ment and sets up instead in the popular Box alignment, then we also have excellent possession possibilities. Against a team that sets up in the Box alignment at the mid-court area, we attempt to tip the basketball back into the back court. The safety valve of the "Y" alignment will be the receiver whenever we tip the basketball back into the back court (Diagram 121, preceding page).

This deep tip maneuver into the back court and near the opponent's goal is dangerous. However, with practice and hard work, this tipping maneuver will add numerous possessions from the jump ball situations.

NOTE: In utilizing this maneuver it is important that the jumper (5) and the deep man (1) have hand and foot signals between them so that they both will know where the basketball will be tipped.

For the jump ball situations that occur at either free-throw circle, we utilize the Box alignment (Diagram 122).

The reason we set up in the Box alignment instead of the "Y" alignment at the free-throw circles is that we feel this alignment offers us better coverage from these particular floor areas. We have experimented with the "Y" alignment at both free-throw circles and found it to be impractical.

We will discuss the Box alignment at both the opponent's free-throw circle and from our own free-throw circle.

Diagram 123 illustrates the Box alignment whenever a jump ball takes place in our offensive court.

5 sets up as the jumper; 4 and 3 (our big men) line up inside and are our primary receivers. 2 and 1 are our defensive safety valves.

Whenever we have an offensive tipping advantage in our offensive end of the court we will attempt to tip inside to either 4 or 3. In tipping to 4 or 3, we will tip inside to different spots designated by signals from the player who is jumping inside the circle.

In the event we do not have an advantage in the jump ball situation in our offensive end of the court, we will shuttle. Whenever we shuttle during a jump ball situation, we are simply rotating our players in a clockwise or counter-clockwise direction in an attempt to gain possession of the basketball.

When we shuttle in our offensive end of the court, it will be in a counter-clockwise direction. The counter-clockwise rotation of players at the offensive end of the court enables us to rotate toward the jumper who has the advantage tipping hand (Diagram 124).

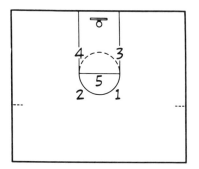

Diagram 122

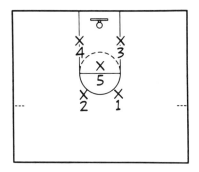

Diagram 123

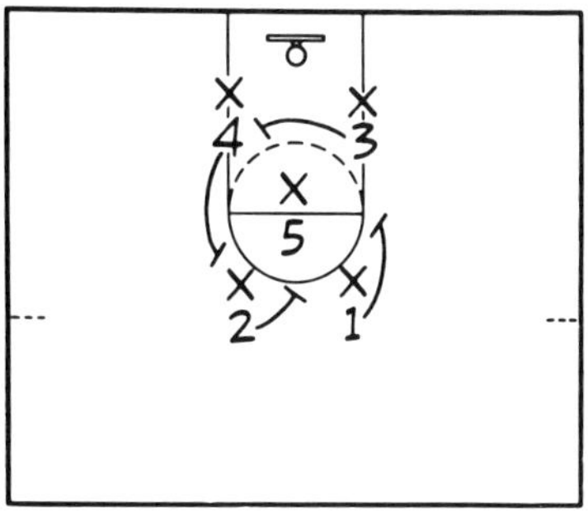

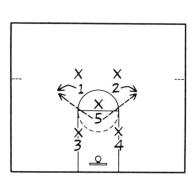

Diagram 124

Diagram 125

NOTE: In executing the shuttle maneuver, it is important that the players hold their positions until the official tosses the basketball into the air. By holding their positions until the ball is tossed into the air the rotating players do not give themselves away to the opposing jumper. This has been a very successful jump ball maneuver for us and has given us possession in situations where we were at a disadvantage.

Diagram 125 illustrates the Box alignment whenever a jump ball takes place in our opponent's court.

Whenever we have a tipping advantage in our opponent's offensive court, we attempt to tip the basketball out and away from their goal. We instruct our jumper never to tip the basketball behind him underneath our opponent's goal. 1 and 2 are our primary receivers, and they must be alert to be able to move laterally to pick up tips to either side of the floor.

If we are at a tipping disadvantage in our opponent's offensive end of the court, we will utilize the shuttle maneuver in this situation. In this jump ball situation, we will shuttle in a clockwise direction (Diagram 126).

The direction in which we shuttle will be dictated in most instances by the jumper who has the tipping advantage. We will key on his tipping hand, usually his right hand, and we will shuttle in that direction.

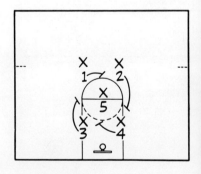

Diagram 126

6

Offensive Stunting with the Flip-Flop

The ability of any offensive pattern in basketball to adjust to changing defensive situations from season to season is of paramount importance in its success. The flexibility of the offensive system, coordinated with the imagination of the coaching staff, can develop new wrinkles and offensive stunts. These wrinkles and stunts are necessary to combat the "stunting" defenses and the changing of the offensive talents of individual players.

The Flip-Flop Offense offers the coaching staff a wide range of offensive adjustments and an almost endless amount of flexibility. By making only a few minor adjustments and alterations in the offense from season to season, we have been able to offset any of the defensive gimmicks our opponents have used against us.

Many of these new "wrinkles" have been picked up at summer coaching clinics in talking with other coaches about their offenses and incorporating their ideas into the Flip-Flop. On other occasions our own players have made constructive suggestions on ways to improve the Flip-Flop, and we have evaluated their suggestions and utilized many of their ideas in our offensive plans.

In the diagrams that follow are some of the offensive adjustments we have made in the Flip-Flop Offense over the years to counter certain defensive situations, as well as to take advantage of the talents of individual players. Since we realize these variations are by no means the only ones that can be added to the Flip-Flop, we are constantly looking for new offensive ideas each season.

TAKING THE DEFENSIVE "BIG MAN" OUTSIDE

One of our most successful offensive adjustments during the past few seasons has been our ability to maneuver the big defensive post men we have faced outside and away from the basket. This particular offensive stunt has also been effective when we have encountered trouble with a strong-side forward defensive overplay.

Diagram 127 illustrates the technique we have utilized in maneuvering the defensive post man outside. Strong-side forward 3 and high-post man 4 line up in a "stack" alignment at the side of the free-throw lane.

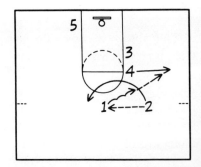

Diagram 127

Guard 2 passes to 1 and executes a guard "hook-back" maneuver; 1 dribbles toward the "stack" attempting to make the guard-to-forward pass. High-post man 4 times his move and steps out to the strong-side forward position to receive the pass from 1 taking the defensive post man with him. After high-post 4 has executed his quick move out to the strong-side forward position, F³ will step up and fill the high-post position. In moving high-post man 4 instead of the forward out to the strong-side forward position to receive the pass from the guard, we are accomplishing two things. First, we are maneuvering the big defensive post man out on the floor and away from the basket; second, we are neutralizing the defensive forward's overplay of our forward by stepping the high-post man out to receive the pass from the guard.

Diagram 128 illustrates the completion of our high-post man outside maneuver.

NOTE: The high-post man must time his move out to the forward position at the exact instant G^1 is in position to pass to him.

To add to the effectiveness of this maneuver, we will alternate F^3 and high-post 4 in stepping them out to receive the pass from G^1. This is keyed by 3, the low man on the stack, who will tag or touch high-post 4 on the leg whenever he wants him to step out to the strong-side forward position to receive the pass from G^1. If F^3 does not use the tag, then he will step out to the strong-side forward position for the pass as in the regular Flip-Flop pattern.

FLASHING THE OFFENSIVE GUARD
INTO THE PIVOT

We have been fortunate in the past to have guards on our ball clubs who have had the size and the inside offensive moves to operate effectively from the pivot position. When we have had guards with these capabilities on our ball club, we have tried to utilize them and integrate them into the Flip-Flop Offense.

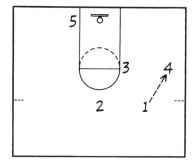

Diagram 128

Another important point to remember is that many teams are still using the little guard because of his speed and quickness. The smart basketball coach, however, when playing against a team using a little guard and employing a man-to-man defense, will neutralize the little guard's speed and quickness by sending the offensive guard he is guarding under the basket and working the ball to him. A small defensive guard in many instances may be very tough defensively when guarding outside on the perimeter of the defense, but he may be unable to defend inside underneath the goal. This inability may be due mainly to his lack of size or his lack of practice and experience in defending underneath the basket.

Diagram 129 illustrates an option we have utilized in past seasons to flash an offensive guard underneath the basket.

Guard 2 passes to F^3 and makes an inside cut to the basket, weak-side forward 5 widens out to a strong-side forward position. After making his cut, G^2 sets up a low post with a little guard under the basket; F^3 dribbles outside and fills G^2's vacated guard spot. F^3 feeds high-post man 4, high-post man 4 faces up to the basket and feeds G^2 as he cuts across underneath the goal with the little defensive guard on his back (Diagram 130).

NOTE: It is important that F^3 does not tip off his pass to high-post man 4 too early by looking at him as he dribbles outside; if he is not deceptive in his maneuvering outside, the defense will sag back

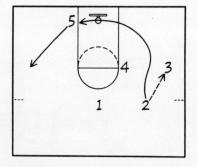

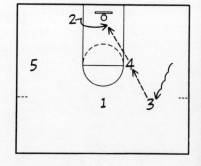

Diagram 129   *Diagram 130*

and prevent him from passing to high-post man 4.

If F^3 is unable to pass to high-post man 4 due to his defensive man's sagging back in front of the high-post area, F^3 can pass to G^1 and execute a "hook-back" maneuver to open up the high-post area for G^1 to feed high-post man 4 (Diagram 131).

In the event G^2 is unable to maneuver for an open shot, we regroup into the Flip-Flop alignment. F^3 clears through after his pass to high-post 4 and sets up a strong-side forward position, 5 moves in and sets up a high-post position, G^1 moves over and sets up a strong-side guard position, high-post 4 drops down and sets up at a weak-side forward position on the baseline, and G^2 rotates out and fills the weak-side guard position at the head of the key (Diagram 132).

The guard to the pivot option is an excellent offensive weapon when used as an integral part of an offensive system without becoming static in movement.

THE BASELINE ADJUSTMENT

The baseline adjustment is an excellent maneuver to use to keep the pressure defenses off balance. This option will enable the offensive guards to penetrate the defense and on many occasions go all the way for the lay-up.

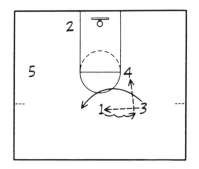

Diagram 131

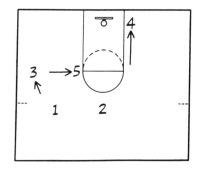

Diagram 132

Diagram 133 illustrates the offensive alignment for the baseline option.

You will notice that strong-side forward 3, high-post 4 and weak-side forward 5 have set up their initial positions on the baseline. This baseline alignment will open up the floor area for G^1 and G^2 to maneuver their defensive men. This alignment has taken away the "sag" and the help from the defensive forwards and center. The defensive guards, without this help from their teammates, will not be able to pressure our guards as effectively.

In the event G^1 and G^2 are not able to score or maneuver for an open shot, then our baseline men will break out to their Flip-Flop position to initiate the offense (Diagram 134).

NOTE: The baseline option's effectiveness is minimized if used too often during the course of a game. It should be utilized only as

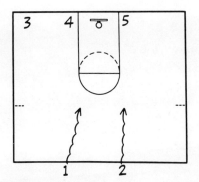

Diagram 133

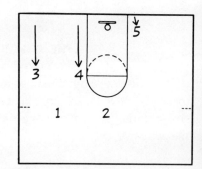

Diagram 134

a surprise formation in order to keep the defensive guards off balance and to open up the center of the court when it becomes congested with sagging defensive men.

DOUBLE SCREENING OPTIONS WITH THE FLIP-FLOP

The double screen is an excellent offensive option that has been incorporated into many modern offenses. It is a particularly effective option whenever a team has an adept jump shooter who does not possess the necessary offensive moves to free himself in a one-on-one situation. We have utilized the double screen on occasion in past seasons, depending upon our personnel and their shooting ability.

Diagram 135 illustrates our first double screening option. This particular screen is set up in an attempt to free an offensive guard for a jump shot at the side of the key.

G^2 passes to G^1 and cuts down the lane; 5, upon seeing G^2's pass and cut down the lane, moves across the lane and sets up a double screen with high-post man 4, G^1, upon receiving G^2's pass, dribbles toward G^2's vacated position in order to draw the defense away from the double screen. He then executes a dribble pivot maneuver and passes back to F^3, who passes to G^2 for a jump shot behind the double screen set by 4 and 5 at the side of the lane.

NOTE: G^1, in executing his dribble and dribble pivot maneuver, will succeed in drawing the defense away from the double screen

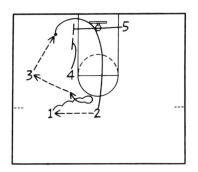

Diagram 135

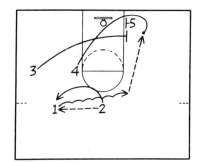

Diagram 136

and will greatly improve the timing and execution of this double screen option.

Diagram 136 illustrates the double screening option for the pivot man. We have used this option in the past to set up our pivot man who was a good jump shooter and to whom we were unable to feed the ball inside due to sagging defenses.

G^1 signals for F^3 to clear across the lane, and F^3 sets up a double screen after his clear-out at the side of the lane with low-post 5. G^2 clears through on a shallow "hook-back" route, G^1 dribbles toward G^2's cleared-out area, high-post man 4 rolls down the lane and rubs his defensive man off on the double screen set up by F^3

and 5 at the side of the lane. G^1 passes to high-post man 4 behind the double screen for a short jump shot.

Whenever we utilize the double screening options, we regroup to get back into the Flip-Flop alignment rather than by flowing back into our regular pattern. The congestion of offensive players at the site of the double screen forces us to regroup rather than to flow back to the opposite side of the floor.

THE TRIPLE SCREEN

The triple screen, when incorporated into the Flip-Flop Offense, can serve as a twofold offensive threat. It can furnish good protection for the close-range jump shot and can open up an excellent one-on-one situation for our high-post man. It is an excellent offensive maneuver to set up in order to take advantage of a good short-range jump shooter. We have also utilized it in the past to work on opposing pivot men who are in foul trouble, by creating a one-on-one situation with them and driving them to the basket.

Diagram 137 illustrates one triple screening maneuver. G^2 passes to weak-side forward 5 and cuts to the basket looking for a return pass, as in our weak-side option. If G^2 does not receive a return

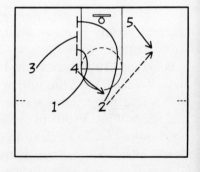

Diagram 137

pass, he sets up on the baseline by the side of the foul lane. F^3 closes in and sets up directly in front of G^2 at the side of the lane. G^1 times his move and, when seeing that G^2 does not receive a return pass from 5, goes inside and sets a screen for high-post man 4, who comes over the top of G^1's screen to the head of the key. G^1, after setting his screen, forms the third man of the triple screen at the side of the lane with G^2 and F^3.

Often high-post man 4 will be open at the head of the key area for a pass from 5 and a jump shot. This situation results from high-post 4's defensive man sagging in the lane too far trying to help defense G^2 on his cut to the basket. Diagram 138 illustrates the triple screen alignment after G^2's initial cut to the basket.

After high-post 4 cuts to the top of the key, 5 passes to high-post 4 and cuts to the basket down the baseline and around the triple screen set at the side of the foul lane. High-post 4 times his move, dribbles toward the screen, and passes to 5 who receives the pass behind the triple screen for the close-range jump shot (Diagram 139).

Diagram 140 illustrates the one-on-one situation high-post man 4 has at the top of the key. High-post man 4, after receiving the pass from 5, holds until 5 has cleared across behind the triple screen; high-post man 4 then takes the defensive pivot man one-on-one into 5's cleared-out area.

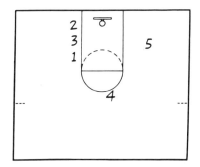

Diagram 138

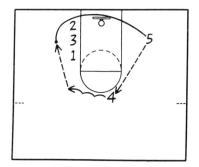

Diagram 139

In the event we are unable to free 5 for a jump shot behind the triple screen or work high-post man 4 loose on the one-on-one situation, we will regroup into the Flip-Flop alignment. The regrouping from the triple screen position into the Flip-Flop alignment is somewhat awkward, and we will not be able to flow back into the basic offensive positions as smoothly as we could with some of the other options.

UTILIZING THE "WEAVE" WITH THE FLIP-FLOP

The "weave" is one of the most popular offensive options in basketball today and is utilized by coaches all over the country. The simplicity of the weave, combined with its constant movement, helps to make it a difficult maneuver for most defenses to contain.

We have utilized the weave on many occasions in conjunction with the Flip-Flop Offense and have found it to be very effective. In most instances, teams will utilize the weave as either a ball control type of pattern or simply as a surprise weapon trying to spring a new offensive wrinkle at the defense. We, ourselves, have utilized the weave with the Flip-Flop more as a surprise weapon. We have found, however, that the weave is an excellent option to call on whenever we are static and bogged down with our offensive movement. It gives us the movement on the ball that we need to put pressure on

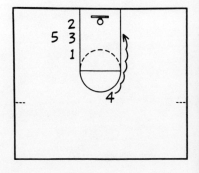

Diagram 140

the defense. Many times, we have found our basic Flip-Flop options to be more successful whenever we have run them after first using the weave option.

Diagram 141 illustrates the weave we have utilized during past seasons.

G^1 begins the weave by dribbling the ball across to G^2 and handing the ball off to him; after G^1 hands the ball off to G^2, he then fills G^2's vacated weak-side guard position. G^2, after receiving the hand-off from G^1, dribbles down to F^3 at the forward position, hands the ball off to F^3, and then fills his strong-side forward position. High-post man 4 and weak-side forward 5 interchange positions and are constantly looking for an opening inside the defense and an opportunity to score. The weave may continue until an opening is found in the defense or another option is set up to run.

NOTE: An important technique to remember in teaching the weave is that after each hand-off the offensive player with the ball takes the ball into his defensive man and attempts to push the defense back toward the basket, thus opening up opportunities for medium-range jump shots.

CHECKING DEFENSIVE STUNTS WITH THE FLIP-FLOP

Many teams today are employing defensive stunts and changing

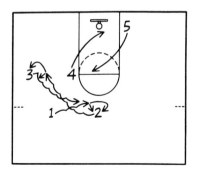

Diagram 141

defenses as surprise weapons attempting to neutralize a team's offensive patterns. A team must be able to recognize these stunts and "wildcat" defenses in order to be successful against them.

One of the most effective methods of "checking" or determining a team's defense is by sending cutters through the defense and rotating the inside pivot men. This is the offensive checking system we use with the Flip-Flop whenever we are uncertain of the defense a team is employing against us. First, we send a guard through the defense to the baseline. This move will determine whether or not the defensive guards are in a man-to-man coverage or a zone coverage. Second, we roll our high-post man down the lane to the basket. This move will check the interior defense and tell us whether or not it is in a man-to-man coverage or a combination coverage.

Diagram 142 illustrates our offensive checking system in determining a team's defenses. G^1 passes to F^3 and cuts through the defense to the baseline. In the event the defensive guard follows G^1 on his cut, then the defensive guards are in a man-to-man coverage. If the defensive guards do not follow G^1 through, then the guards are using zone coverage.

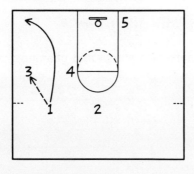

Diagram 142

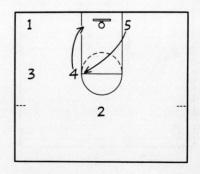

Diagram 143

After determining the coverage of the defensive guards, we will rotate our pivot men to determine the coverage of the interior of the defense. Diagram 143 illustrates the pivot rotation we run to determine the type of interior defense a team is using against us.

High-post man 4 rolls down the lane to the basket and sets up a post position on the baseline. Low-post man 5 holds until high-post 4 has rolled down the lane, then cuts through the heart of the defense up to the high-post position (Diagram 144).

NOTE: If the defensive pivot men follow 4 and 5 on their post rotation routes, then the defensive post men are in a man-to-man coverage; if they do not follow them all the way, then they are in a zone coverage.

We are now in a four-man overload alignment with a point man. By setting up this four-man overload, we have flooded one side of the floor and forced the defense to make some type of adjustment. We will rotate from this four-man overload alignment back into our Flip-Flop formation by clearing F[3] through the defense and setting him up at a strong-side forward position on the opposite side of the floor (Diagram 145).

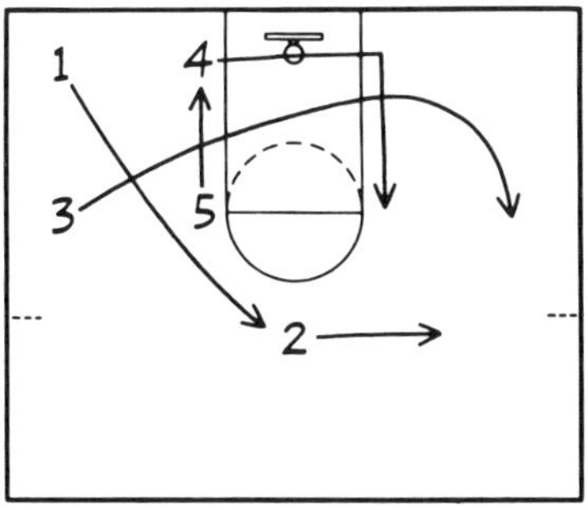

Diagram 145

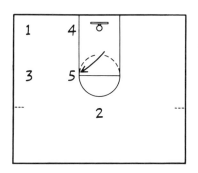

Diagram 144

From the baseline, 4 moves across the lane and up to the high-post position, 5 drops down from the high post and sets up on the baseline, 2 slides over from the weak-side guard position, and 1 moves out from the corner and sets up at a weak-side guard.

We are now in our Flip-Flop alignment, having checked the defense for its coverage, and we are now ready to offense it accordingly (Diagram 146).

This method of checking defenses and determining an opposing team's defensive coverage has given us excellent offensive movement. Against teams that have played us combination defense, this checking movement has given us excellent scoring opportunities.

DOUBLE-POSTING WITH THE FLIP-FLOP

The integration of the double-post alignment on occasion into the Flip-Flop affords us an excellent offensive element of surprise. By simply moving the weak-side forward up the lane and setting him up even with the free-throw line extended and directly across from the high-post man, we are able to go into a double-post alignment.

This particular double-post stunt has been effective for us against those teams that have attempted to overplay our high-post man. Defensive high-post overplay has in some instances been troublesome to the Flip-Flop due to the congestion of the lane area. The defensive player guarding the high-post man can afford to gamble and overplay the high-post man knowing that he will be backed up by his defensive teammate who is guarding the weak-side forward (Diagram 147).

Notice that high-post man 4's defensive man is playing him high and has cut off his passing lane from the guards. Weak-side forward 5's defensive man is sagging in the lane area helping to prevent any lob pass to the high-post man from the outside.

When first encountering this defensive overplay, we counteracted it with the post rotation pattern of the Flip-Flop illustrated in Chapter 1 of this book. After a while we discovered that the post rotation pattern by itself was not always enough to counteract the high-post overplay; consequently, we experimented with the double-post alignment and produced this double-post pattern.

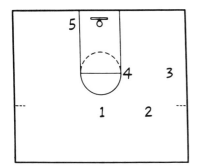   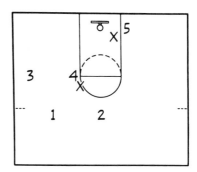

Diagram 146   *Diagram 147*

Our double-post stunt against a defensive high-post overplay is illustrated in Diagram 148.

Notice weak-side forward 5 has set the double-post pattern up by moving up to a high-post position across high-post man 4. 5's defensive man must come high with him to prevent 5 from taking an easy short-range jump shot from the free-throw line. High-post man 4 and weakside forward 5 are both lined up even with the foul lane extended. You will note this has opened up the area underneath the basket taking away the defensive congestion in the lower lane area.

Diagram 149 illustrates the "lob" pass maneuver from our double-post alignment. Strong-side guard 1 fakes a short pass to high-post man 4 attempting to draw the high-post man's defensive man higher and make him overcommit himself in his overplay; if he is successful in doing this, then high-post man 4 rolls quickly toward the basket and G^1 feeds him a high lob pass underneath the basket. This "lob" pass will be successful only once, maybe twice, in a game, but it will definitely help to keep the defensive high-post man honest.

Diagram 150 illustrates the second option from our double-post alignment.

Strong-side guard 1 has the ball and feeds G^2, G^2 feeds the ball to the weak-side forward (5) who has moved up the lane to set up a double-post position. High-post man 4, upon seeing 5 receive the ball at the double-post position, quickly pivots and breaks via the back-door route underneath the basket. If high-post man 4 is open underneath the goal on his back-door cut, then 5 will feed him the

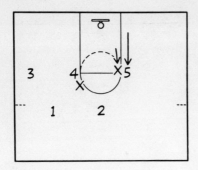

Diagram 148

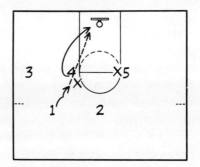

Diagram 149

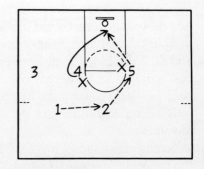

Diagram 150

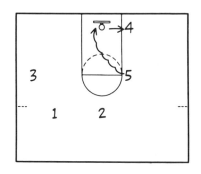 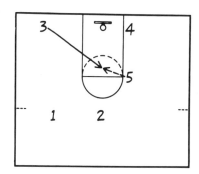

Diagram 151   *Diagram 152*

ball. Many times a high-post man's defensive man will relax or take his eye from his man when a pass is made away from him to an opposite post man. Whenever the defensive man commits these unpardonable defensive sins, we can score easy baskets by the back-door cut to the basket.

Diagram 151 illustrates one of the secondary offensive opportunities in the event that high-post man 4 is not open on his back-door cut to the basket.

5 faces the basket looking for high-post man 4. If 4 is not open underneath, he continues across the lane and sets up at a low-post position. This maneuver has cleared the lane area and opened it up for 5 to dribble to his left down the lane for a driving lay-up. Notice that strong-side forward 3 has to keep his defensive man occupied by taking him down low to the baseline.

Diagram 152 illustrates the final option of our double-post pattern. Weak-side forward 5 has the ball and is unable to free himself for a shot; weak-side forward 3 times his move from the baseline where he has carried his defensive man and breaks up through the lane for a pass from 5 and a short-range shot.

This option is excellent for a forward who is a good one-on-one basketball player. The lane area is open and offers the forward more than ample room to work on his defensive man. We have set up this particular option in some instances when we wanted to work on a certain forward one-on-one and attempt to get him into foul trouble.

After we have run this option a few times, we then go to our guard back-door cut option (Diagram 153).

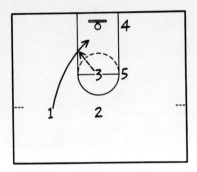

Diagram 153

Strong-side guard 1, upon seeing weak-side forward 3 receive the ball, checks his own defensive man. If his defensive man has relaxed or turned his head to watch weak-side forward 3 receive the ball, then 1 cuts via the back-door route to the basket. Weak-side forward 3 looks for 1 on his back-door cut to the basket and feeds 1 for a lay-up. A bounce pass will in most instances be the most effective pass to feed 1 on his back-door cut to the basket.

Diagram 154 illustrates the rotation for our completed double-post pattern.

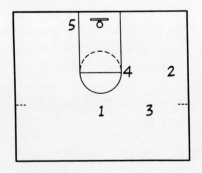

Diagram 154

2 moves down and fills a strong-side forward position, 4 moves up from the baseline and sets up at the high-post position, 3 steps out and fills the strong-side guard position, 5 rolls down the lane and sets up at a weak-side forward position, and 1, after his back-door cut to the basket, flows back out and sets up at a weak-side guard position.

The stunts and adjustments we have discussed in this chapter are offensive wrinkles we have incorporated into the Flip-Flop Offense at one time or another. We have utilized these stunts to keep our opponents off balance and to help combat a particular opponent's rigged defenses against our pattern type of offense. Let me emphasize to you that these are stunts we have utilized over a period of several seasons, and we have never used all of these stunts or adjustments during a single season. A sound coaching philosophy concerning the stunts and adjustments discussed in this chapter would be to study and evaluate advantages and disadvantages of each of these stunts. The coach should also analyze to what extent his personnel can utilize these stunts to full advantage.

A surprise offensive tactic we have used in the past for important tournament or conference games is the insertion of one of these particular offensive stunts the first four or five minutes of the first half to keep an opponent off balance defensively. This maneuver tends to cut down on the defensive aggressiveness of our opponents and helps to set them up for the "kill" when we flow into our Flip-Flop pattern.

7

The Flip-Flop and
the Controlled Break

The fast break is the greatest offensive weapon in the game of basketball today. It offers a team a countless number of easy baskets during the course of a game. The fast break when utilized effectively is exciting and colorful and offers the spectators a thrilling run and shoot type of game.

The renewed interest in, and rise in popularity of, professional basketball with its run and shoot style of play has helped to promote the use of the fast break by coaches all over the nation. Many of the coaches today will utilize the fast break as their primary offensive weapon, gearing their entire offensive and defensive system around the fast break. To be *consistently* successful its execution requires great skill and finesse on the part of the players.

THE CONTROLLED BREAK

During my high school coaching tenure at Dekalb County High School, I utilized a fire-house run and shoot type of fast break system. In this system the players simply filled the fast break lanes with no organized prearranged fast break pattern. After an unsuccessful break there was no organized regrouping into the regular offense. Although my teams at Dekalb County enjoyed success with this fast break system, I fully realized the weaknesses of this un-organized scramble type of system.

When I went to Martin Junior College as head basketball coach, I set out to establish an organized controlled type of break system with a definite set of rules: Rules to govern both the initial break and the regrouping from the break into our basic offense, the Flip-Flop. After installing a controlled break system at Martin College and coordinating it with the Flip-Flop Offense, the success we enjoyed during the four seasons there was phenomenal. The Martin College basketball team during the next four years won three Dixie Conference Championships, two invitational tournaments, and in the fourth season was ranked eighth in the final national junior college poll. Much of this success can be credited to the Flip-Flop and the controlled break system.

THE BASIC ESSENTIALS OF THE CONTROLLED BREAK

Before installing any type of offensive breaking system it is important that the coaching staff drill the players daily in the basic essentials of the break. These basic essentials are the fundamentals that each player must develop by repetition in the daily practice sessions. The following are the Eight Basic Essentials for the break:

The first basic essential is the development of the defensive rebounding triangle. Blocking-out on the defensive board is the most important single factor in teaching a running type of offensive system. Aggressiveness in rebounding will in many instances help to offset a lack of great jumping ability.

In teaching the blocking-out technique on the defensive board, there are several conflicting theories concerning the proper technique to use. Some coaches stress the teaching of the reverse pivot block-out technique; other coaches teach the cross-over block-out technique. A few coaches do not teach the block-out and instruct their players to go for the ball and ignore the block-out.

We teach our forwards the cross-over step technique in blocking-out and instruct our centers to use the reverse-pivot technique. Our forwards utilize the cross-over technique because of the wide floor area they have to cover, and it also enables them to maintain visual contact with their opponent while blocking-out. Our centers utilize the reverse-pivot technique because of the small lane area they have to cover and also because it does not require the speed and the quickness of the cross-over step.

In executing the cross-over step technique, the defensive forward quickly drops back one step when the shot is taken, influencing the offensive forward to the middle of the floor. When the offensive forward attempts to go to the board toward the middle of the floor, we teach our forwards to swing their outside foot nearest the side-lines, across in front of the offensive forward. This cross-over movement will swing the forward's entire body around between the offensive forward and the basket. If the offensive forward goes to the board down the baseline, then the defensive forward will cross over with his inside foot and swing his body in that direction. By utilizing the cross-over technique, our forwards are able to maintain visual contact on their opponent during the initial phase of the blocking-out maneuver.

Maintaining visual contact on an opponent is of paramount importance. In most instances, whenever a forward fails to block his opponent off the board it is due to the loss of visual contact. The wide floor area that our forwards have to defend requires us to utilize the cross-over step technique.

Our centers utilize the reverse-pivot technique in blocking the offensive post men off of the board. This particular blocking-out technique is easy to execute by a defensive post man. It does not require the quickness that it takes to execute the cross-over step, and we have found that it offers the defensive post man better body balance during the block-out. Generally speaking, the center does not possess the speed and the quickness of the other players and he must compensate for this.

The defensive post man, with his body weight distributed low, pivots on the foot nearest the offensive post man's cut to the board; as the defensive post man pivots, he quickly swings his other leg around in a clockwise rotation in front of the offensive post man. This movement when executed correctly will offer the defensive post man good body balance, with weight distributed low, and a quicker technique so necessary in blocking-out a post man positioned close to the basket.

In developing the correct form by our forwards and centers for both the cross-over step and the reverse-pivot block techniques, it is imperative that we emphasize these techniques daily. In our preseason practice sessions we devote from ten to fifteen minutes daily on the block-out. Much of this preseason practice time allotted to teaching the block-out is devoted to dummy drills (no contact) and corrective teaching. During our regular season practice sessions we devote from five to eight minutes daily exclusively for the block-out. This time is devoted to one-on-one, three-on-three, and five-on-five half-court block-out drills. Aggressiveness is emphasized during these block-out drills, and we stress good strong body contact in these practice sessions.

The "jack-knife" technique in rebounding is the second basic essential in developing the offensive break. After blocking-out on the defensive board, the player jumps and gains possession of the basketball, executing the "jack-knife" technique. This technique is executed with the player jumping high with his arms extended, his feet spread widely apart and extended out, and his rear end extended backward into his opponent. In executing the "jack-knife" the player's body is in the shape of a V with his arms and feet extended outward and his rear end extended backward. We have found that teaching the "jack-knife" technique is not only an excellent method for obtaining a defensive rebound, but also for protecting the rebound after possession.

The outlet pass is the third essential of the break. The outlet pass is the "trigger" of the break. The quickness and the accuracy with which the outlet pass is made will go a long way in determining the success of the break. We teach two types of outlet passes, the hook pass and the two-hand over-head pass. The hook pass should be used whenever a player is pressured to prevent the outlet pass. We teach the rebounder to step away from the pressure and hook the ball, as in shooting a hook shot, out to start the break. The two-hand over-head pass is an excellent pass to use in "flipping" the ball out at the peak of the jump to start the break.

Both of these outlet passes should be thrown to the receiver chest high and outside to the receiver. The outlet pass should not be a "lob" type of pass but should be a sharp, line drive pass.

The fourth basic essential is the filling of the break lanes. The middle lane and the two outside lanes should be filled in order to have good floor balance on the break. An organized system for filling the lanes will better insure a team's consistency in filling the break lanes. The front three offensive penetrators, who have filled the break lanes, should stay wide in order to prevent the defenders from double-teaming the offensive player with the ball.

The fifth basic essential is to "pass first, then dribble." The dribble only tends to slow down the initial break; consequently, we instruct our players to dribble only as a last resort in starting the break. After the break has started and the ball is in the middle lane, then the dribble is more desirable than the pass. The bounce pass should not be used at any time during the break except by the middle man at the completion of the break in passing to a cutter. There will be exceptions to this rule in situations where a player will be forced to utilize the dribble rather than the pass. However, we have found that by indoctrinating our players with this rule, it has helped to speed up our break and has cut down on floor violations.

The sixth basic essential is "Do not fight defensive pressure." The player with the basketball during the break should not fight defensive pressure. Defensive pressure tends to slow or "bog" down the break. The player with the ball should be instructed always to move the ball away from defensive pressure during any phase of the break. In defending against the break, the defense will be instructed to stop the ball. It is imperative that the ball be advanced beyond these defenders. Many times the break is stymied by the offensive player with the ball attempting to outmaneuver a defender who is pressuring him. Instead of attempting to outmaneuver the defender, he should pass the ball up the court to an unguarded teammate.

A cardinal offensive principle in advancing the ball against pressure defenders is to hunt openings in the defense. This principle also definitely applies to the break, where it is important to pass always to the open man.

Utilizing the trailer is the seventh basic essential of the break. The trailer is the fourth offensive player down the floor on the break. The first three offensive players down the floor fill the break lanes and are known as the front-line penetrators. The trailer, the fourth offensive player down the floor, fills a trailing lane behind the front-line penetrators. The side of the floor on which he comes down depends upon the side of the floor on which the ball was passed out to start the break. This rule helps to simplify the trailers' routes on the break.

On many occasions, the defense may be successful in defending against the three front-line penetrators of the break but unable to contain the trailer. The trailer when utilized off the break will be open for many short- to medium-range jump shots.

The eighth basic essential is to "maintain defensive floor balance" with the break. This simply means that the offensive players on the break should always be ready to revert quickly to defense.

The rebounder who started the break is the "safety valve." In most instances, he will stay back and will not participate in the break.

The trailer, who trails along behind the break, should be ready to retreat into the defensive court and help the player who is the "safety valve" on defense.

Maintaining defensive floor balance may be referred to as the defensive break. The "defensive break" should be emphasized when installing the offensive break. The offensive players involved in the break must be ready at all times to convert back to defense.

THE FOUR P'S OF THE CONTROLLED BREAK

1. Possession
   a. "Fight to gain possession of the ball and concentrate to maintain possession." Each possession is worth ½ of a point.
   b. Possession may be gained by deflection, steal, interception, score by opponents, or any violation.

2. Position
   a. Block-out on the defensive board
   b. Carry out offensive assignments on the break by filling the assigned lanes, clearing out, exploiting the defensive openings.

3. Poise
   a. Maintain good body balance at all times. Never run out of control.
   b. Advance the ball quickly but with an air of caution.
   c. Thrive on pressure; invite the defense to challenge you before passing off to a teammate.

4. Percentage shot
   a. Take only the high percentage shot from the break.
   b. Run every break as though it were the final minute of the game. You must score or maintain possession of the ball.

The following are rules that govern and discipline the controlled break. These rules give the three front-line penetrators of the break a definite plan of attack.

RULES GOVERNING THE CONTROLLED BREAK

1. Run to half-court on all break situations.
2. At half-court, whenever the offense has the defense outnumbered, take advantage of the break. Whenever the defense outnumbers the offense, set up and run the basic pattern, the Flip-Flop Offense.
3. Use verbal signals to take advantage of the break or set it up: "Go" to run and "Set" to slow down and set up the basic offense. The middle man on the break will control the break with the verbal signal.
4. Do not force the break at half-court if the defense equals the offense. However, take advantage of one-on-one and two-on-two situations. The offensive abilities of the players involved in these situations will determine whether or not the offense will run or set up.
5. Maintain good body control at all times, look for openings, throw the long pass only when absolutely certain.
6. The front three breakers, who fill the middle and outside lanes, should take only the "crip" or the short-range jump shot off the controlled break.
7. Take the medium-range jump shot only when utilizing the trailer.
8. Never take the long-range jump shot off the controlled break.
9. The best opportunity for the controlled break comes from the loose ball. (There is no defense for this break.) Next, in order of preference: from the rebound, free throw, the throw-in out of bounds in back court, and jump balls.

These rules are general rules and apply to most of the break situations. However, the cardinal rule that applies to the controlled break is that when in doubt always set up the basic pattern. Whenever the middle man on the break is in doubt whether to go all the way or set it up, play conservative and set it up. Possession of the basketball is of paramount importance.

COORDINATING THE CONTROLLED BREAK
WITH THE FLIP-FLOP

In coordinating the controlled break with the Flip-Flop Offense, we have combined two offensive scoring weapons and have doubled our scoring opportunities.

After an unsuccessful break we have an organized system of regrouping into our basic offense, the Flip-Flop. This system of regrouping has enabled our players to fill the Flip-Flop floor positions with ease rather than having to scramble to get into the basic offense.

The idea of an organized system of regrouping into the basic offense off an unsuccessful break came to me several years ago. Following years of observing basketball teams scrambling around and clumsily attempting to get back into their basic offense after unsuccessful fast break situations, I suddenly realized that an organized controlled type of break with definite rules for regrouping into the basic offense would add to the effectiveness of both the break and the basic offense.

Many of the coaches today who are advocates of the fast break do not utilize organized fast break patterns. These coaches adhere to the theory of "first come first served," which means they instruct their players to simply run and locate a lane to fill. This type of unorganized break can be successful for those coaches who have the quick players that are good ball handlers and passers. However, for the coaches who do not have the outstanding players or the coaches who play the percentages in basketball and want to cut down on the turnovers, organized break patterns are the answer. Patterns designed to score from a break situation when properly executed will produce many easy baskets.

The diagrams that follow illustrate some of our controlled break patterns designed to score the quick basket. These diagrams also illustrate our organized regrouping off an unsuccessful break into our basic offense, the Flip-Flop.

NOTE: The following break patterns are from a two-guard defensive front, as this is the defensive front from which we find ourselves starting our break most of the time.

OFF-SIDE GUARD TO THE MIDDLE

The first controlled break pattern we shall discuss is probably one of the oldest, most popular patterns used today. We call the pattern, "off-side guard to the middle," meaning just what it says—the guard away from the ball comes to the middle for a pass to lead the break (Diagram 155).

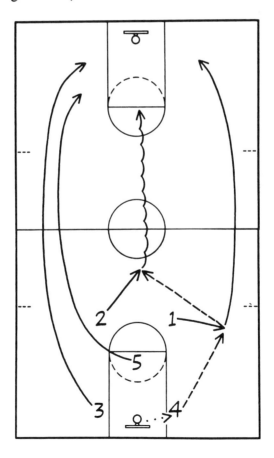

Diagram 155

4, 5, and 3 have established the defensive rebounding triangle. 4 either rebounds the ball off the defensive board, or after a made field goal he steps out of bounds with the ball, and passes out to the guard (1) on his side of the court; 2, the off-side guard, breaks to the middle lane for a pass from 1; 3 breaks out from underneath the basket on the opposite side of the floor and fills the outside lane; 4, who rebounded the ball, will stay back for defense as the "safety valve"; 5 breaks out from directly underneath the basket and becomes the "trailer" on the break and fills the trailing lane behind 3; 2, who handles the ball in the middle, takes the ball to the foul lane and feeds either the outside cutters or the trailer. 2 will on occasion be able to go all the way himself. (We will discuss how we utilize the trailer in a special section of this chapter.)

This particular break pattern will usually be effective in the early part of a ball game while the middle area of the floor is still open. As the game progresses, the middle area of the floor will be guarded in an attempt to shut off the passing lane to the middle and stop the break. Whenever the passing lane is cut off to the middle, then we will run one of our other break patterns.

Diagram 156 illustrates the organized regrouping from an unsuccessful break into the Flip-Flop.

3 breaks out and fills the strong-side forward position; 5, who was the trailer, fills the high-post position; 4 fills the weak-side forward position; 2, who was the middle man on the break, moves over and fills the strong-side guard position; 1 breaks out from the baseline and fills the weak-side guard position. Now we are ready to smoothly initiate the Flip-Flop Offense.

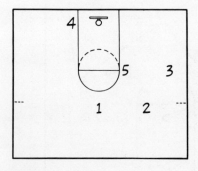

Diagram 156

OFF-SIDE GUARD DEEP

The off-side guard deep pattern on the break is designed to open up the middle area of the floor. In this pattern the off-side guard, instead of cutting to the middle, will go deep looking for the long pass, thus clearing out the middle area of the floor (Diagram 157).

4, 5, and 3 form the defensive rebounding triangle. 4 rebounds the ball. (For purposes of illustrating, we have allowed 4 to rebound the ball to start each pattern. Although these patterns can be run from both sides of the floor, it helps to simplify these break patterns for the readers by allowing 4 to start each break.) 4 flips the ball out to 1 to start the break; the off-side guard 2 goes deep, thus clearing out the middle area of the floor; 3, who was the off-side rebounder on the board, breaks to the cleared-out middle area. 1 can pass either to the middle man (3) or up court to 2. In the event 1 passes

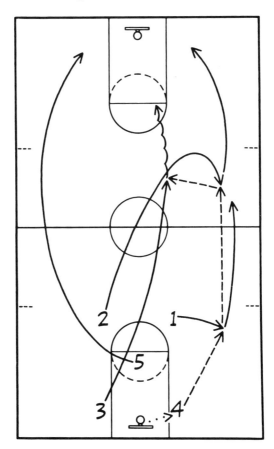

Diagram 157

the ball up court to 2, who has "button-hooked" back for the pass
and for whom we look most of the time after receiving the ball,
2 looks to drive all the way to the basket. If he can go all the way

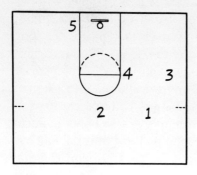

Diagram 158

for the basket, he should do so. If not, he looks to the middle and
passes to 3, who has filled the deep middle lane. 5, who was the
middle rebounder, peels off and fills the opposite outside lane.
1, who passed the ball up court to 2, becomes the trailer, filling
the lane behind 2. 3, the middle man with the ball, dribbles to the
foul lane and feeds either the outside cutters or the trailer. 4, who
rebounded the ball, stays back for defense at the mid-court area. It is
important to the success of the break that the middle man with the
ball penetrate the defense and force the defenders to commit themselves.

Diagram 158 illustrates the organized regrouping after an unsuccessful break into the Flip-Flop.

3 sets up to his right at the strong-side forward position, 4 fills
the high-post position, 5 fills the weak-side forward position, 2, the
guard that went deep or long, moves out to the weak-side guard
position. 1, who was the trailer, fills the strong-side guard position.

BALL-SIDE GUARD DEEP

This particular break pattern is designed to counteract any team
that attempts to stop our outlet pass. One of the most successful
methods of stopping the breaking game of a team is by stopping

or slowing down the outlet pass that starts the break. Generally speaking, it is usually the defensive guards who attempt to overplay the outlet pass. 2 passes up court to 1, who has performed a "hook-back" maneuver. 3 comes down court in the middle lane; 5, the middle rebounder, "peels off" and fills the outside lane on the opposite side of the floor. 2 fills the trailing lane behind 1.

Diagram 159 illustrates the ball-side guard deep break pattern.

Diagram 160 illustrates the organized regrouping from an unsuccessful break into the Flip-Flop.

3, who filled the middle lane, sets up at the strong-side forward position to his right. 4 sets up at the high-post position; 5 sets up at the weak-side forward position; 2 sets up at the strong-side guard position; 1, the deep man on the break, circles out and fills the weak-side guard position.

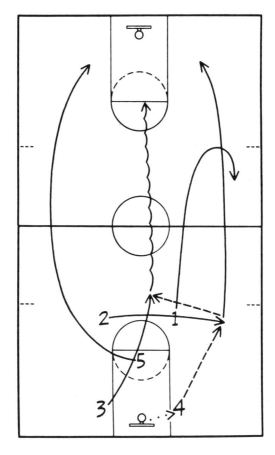

Diagram 159

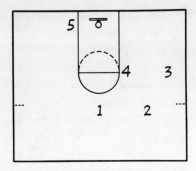

Diagram 160

GUARD SCREEN PATTERN

The guard screen pattern is another excellent break pattern we use to combat the teams that attempt to prevent the outlet pass to start the break. In this particular pattern the guards screen for each other in order to free themselves for the outlet pass. We key this pattern by ruling that whenever the middle rebounder gets the ball the guards will screen for each other in an attempt to shake their defensive men.

NOTE: The rule concerning the guard screen pattern can be removed at any time during a game. You will also note for illustration purposes that in our other break patterns, 4 rebounds the ball to start each break. To initiate the guard screen pattern in actual game situations, 5 must rebound the ball. Diagram 161 illustrates the guard screen break pattern.

4, 5 and 3 form the rebounding triangle. 5 rebounds the ball, and 1 and 2, upon seeing 5 gain possession of the ball, screen for each other. 5 passes to 2; 3, the off-side rebounder, breaks out and fills the middle lane; 2, who has screened for 1, moves outside and fills the outside lane. 4 fills the trailing lane behind 1.

Diagram 162 (next page) illustrates the organized regrouping of an unsuccessful break into the Flip-Flop.

3, the middle man on the break, sets up at a strong-side forward position to his right. 4, the trailer, fills the high-post position; 5 fills the weak-side forward position. 2 moves out and fills the strong-side guard position; 1 moves out and fills the weak-side guard position.

DOUBLE GUARD DEEP PATTERN

The double guard deep pattern is an excellent pattern for a team to use as a surprise attack. This pattern is also good to run whenever the two defensive guards are stopping or slowing down the break. By using the simple maneuver of sending both of our offensive guards deep for the long pass and forcing the defensive guards to follow them, we have taken the defensive guards out of position. From this deep position the defensive guards will be unable to stop the break (Diagram 163).

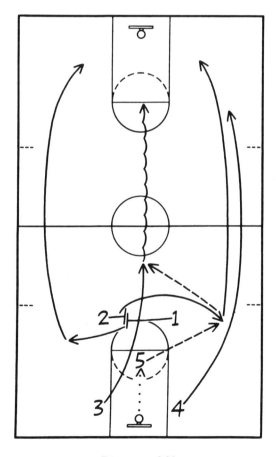

Diagram 161

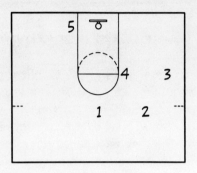

Diagram 162

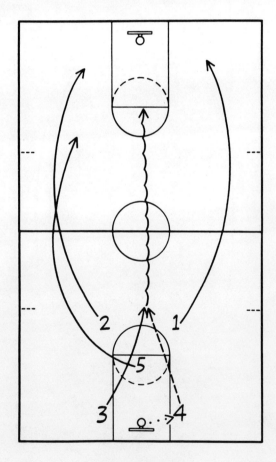

Diagram 163

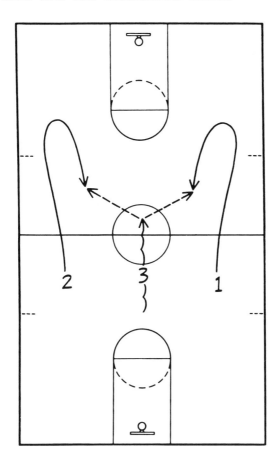

Diagram 164

4, 5, and 3 form the rebounding triangle. 4 rebounds the ball;
1 and 2, upon seeing 4 gain possession of the ball, turn and run at
full speed up court looking for the long pass. If either 1 or 2 is
open, 4 will throw a long pass to him. If neither is open then 3, the
off-side rebounder, cuts right up through the middle of the free-
throw lane; 4 feeds 3 a short pass. 3, afer receiving the outlet pass
from 4, dribbles up court and becomes the middle man in the break.
5, the middle rebounder, becomes the trailer in this pattern filling
the lane behind 2. 5's rule in filling the break lanes is to go opposite
the direction of the outlet pass. If 3, after receiving the outlet pass
from 4, should be pressured while dribbling up court, then 1 and 2

should "button-hook" back for him to pass to (Diagram 164).

Diagram 165 illustrates the organized regrouping off an unsuccessful break into the Flip-Flop.

3, who filled the middle break lane, sets up at the strong-side forward position to his right. 4 sets up at the high-post position. 5, who filled the opposite outside lane, sets up at the weak-side forward position. The guards 1 and 2 both go to the baseline and come out on opposite sides of the floor. 2 sets up at the strong-side guard position, while 1 sets up the weak-side guard position.

THE CONTROLLED BREAK FROM THE FREE THROW

The free-throw situation offers an excellent opportunity to take advantage of the break. There are many break patterns utilized today, but the following pattern is one of the most effective ones.

This particular break pattern from the free throw is a favorite of Coach John Oldham, basketball coach at Western Kentucky, and his teams have scored a great many field goals from it. The theory behind the pattern is based on creating a mismatch with a small defensive guard attempting to guard a tall forward up court (Diagram 166).

The free-throw alignment is as follows: 3, who is the key to the pattern, lines up up court in a deep position. 3 serves as a scoring threat for the long pass up court to him. The opposing team will be forced to assign a player to guard 3 in order to prevent the long pass and an easy basket. In most instances they will assign a small guard to defend against the tall forward. 5 and 4 set up at the inside positions under the basket, 2 lines up at a high foul line position, and he is assigned to block out the shooter. 1 lines up at a wing position behind 4. This free-throw pattern, like the other break patterns, can be run from both successful and unsuccessful goal attempts. For illustration purposes, however, 4 again rebounds the ball and executes an outlet pass to 1. After the outlet pass 4 stays back on defense. 2 breaks to the middle and receives a pass from 1; 1 after passing to 2 in the middle lane fills the outside lane; 5 fills the opposite outside lane. 3, upon seeing 2 advancing the ball across mid-court with 1 and 5 filling the outside lanes, takes his defensive man down to the baseline. This maneuver presents us with two

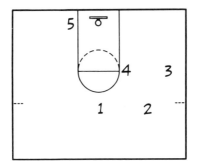

Diagram 165

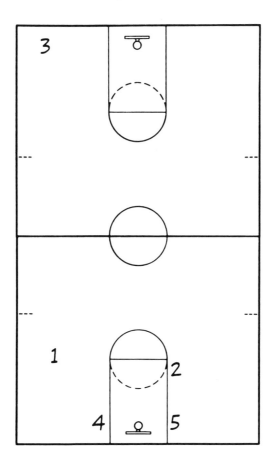

Diagram 166

scoring options: first, we can exploit 3, the tall forward underneath the basket with the little defensive guard on him; second, we can look for a guard to be open for a short- to medium-range jump shot. The offensive guard will be open in most instances due to the fact that one of the defensive guards has been forced to defend against the forward (3) underneath the basket (Diagram 167).

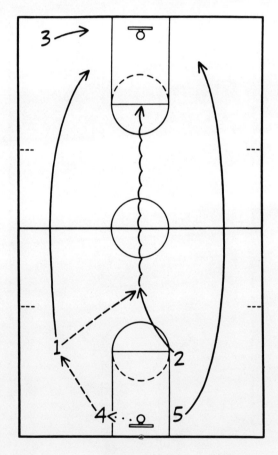

Diagram 167

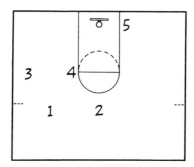

Diagram 168

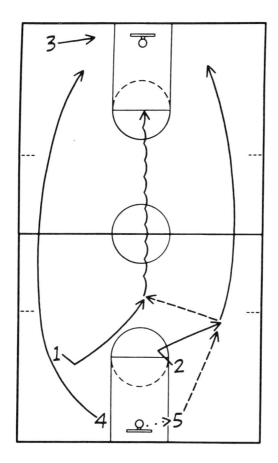

Diagram 169

Diagram 168 illustrates the organized regrouping off an unsuccessful break.

3 sets up at the strong-side forward position; 1 sets up at a strong-side guard position, and 2 sets up at a weak-side guard position. 4 sets up at the high-post position, and 5 sets up at the weak-side forward position.

In the event that the center (5) rebounds the ball instead of 4, then the routes of the players will be changed. The free-throw break patterns are determined by the player who rebounds the ball (Diagram 169).

5 rebounds the ball; 2, who is lined up at the high-foul lane position, breaks out to the side for the outlet pass from 5. 5 passes out to 2 on the side of the court. 1, who is positioned on the opposite side of the court, breaks to the middle of the floor. 2 passes to 1 in the middle lane; 4, the off-side rebounder, fills the opposite outside lane; 3 takes his defensive man low to the baseline. The scoring options are the same in both situations, the only variations are the break routes. The organized regrouping is the same with both options.

UTILIZING THE TRAILER WITH THE BREAK

The trailer, the fourth man down the floor, can be utilized in many different ways. There are several theories concerning the use of the trailer in the break. Some coaches utilize the trailer solely as an offensive rebounder, not as a shooter; that is, they "crash" him to the board. Some coaches "isolate" the trailer at the mid-court area and instruct him to remain there for defensive balance. Other coaches will include the trailer in the break, but will seldom take advantage of him. They will not use him as an offensive threat.

The trailer is an integral part of the controlled break. We will utilize the trailer as the situation arises on the break. On many occasions the defense will be successful in stopping the initial break but unable to contain the trailer.

The trailer will fill the assigned lane directly behind one of the front lane cutters.

Diagram 170 illustrates the floor position of the cutter on the break.

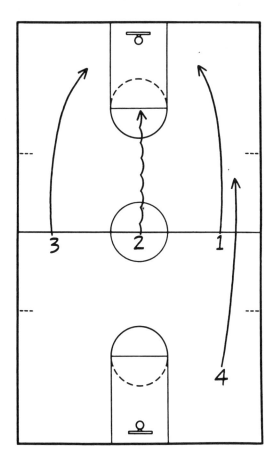

Diagram 170

Notice that 4, the trailer, is filling the trailing lane in the break directly behind 1.

NOTE: This is contrary to the rule to which many teams adhere concerning the cutting route of the trailer. These teams instruct the trailer to fill a lane between the middle man in the break and the player in the outside lane.

We feel that by filling a trailing lane behind one of the front lane cutters the trailer will be in a more advantageous position once inside the scoring area. The maneuver we utilize on the break once the lane cutters penetrate the scoring area will help to "shake" the trailer loose for a short- to medium-range jump shot.

Diagrams 171 and 172 illustrate the maneuver we utilize on the break once we penetrate the defense that helps to free the trailer for a shot.

2, the middle man on the break and the ball handler, dribbles into the scoring area and penetrates the defense; the outside cutters, 1 and 3, cut diagonally to the basket and take the defenders against the break inside to the basket. 4, the trailer, after the front lane cutter 1 has carried the defensive man under the basket, moves quickly to the floor area between the top of the key and the foul

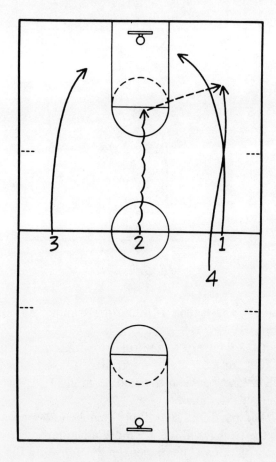

Diagram 171

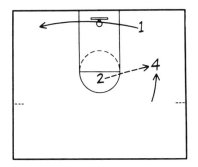

Diagram 172

lane extended. In the event the trailer is open, he verbally signals for the ball from the middle man. We use the verbal signal "trailer" to set up the pass to the trailer.

After the pass is made to the trailer inside the scoring area, the front lane cutter (1) clears out to the other side of the court (Diagram 172). 1, in clearing across to the opposite side of the floor, has opened up the entire right side of the floor for the trailer 4 to operate. This simple clear-out maneuver at the end of the break has produced for us many lay-ups and three point plays.

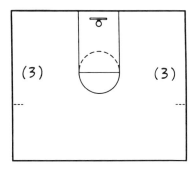

Diagram 173

RESPONSIBILITIES OF THE TRAILER

1. He fills the assigned break lane.
2. He gives the verbal signal when he finds himself open inside the scoring area.
3. He is ready to convert quickly from offense to defense.
4. He, in converting to defense, retreats to the opposite "key" area and stops the ball.
5. He does not force a shot inside the scoring area; if he is covered, chances are one of the front lane cutters is open.
6. He rebounds the high lane area after a shot is taken on the break.

FLIP-FLOP POSITIONS

1. Players will "key" on the strong-side forward (3), the side of the floor he sets up on will, when regrouping, determine their Flip-Flop floor positions.

Diagram 173 illustrates Rule 1 governing our offensive regrouping.

2. Whenever the strong-side forward (3) fills one of the side lanes in the break, he will set up at the strong-side forward position on the same side of the floor. (This rule applies if we decide to break or set it up.)

Diagram 174 illustrates Rule 2 governing our offensive regrouping.

3. Whenever the strong-side forward (3) fills the middle lane of the break, in regrouping he will always set up his strong-side forward position on the side of the floor to his right. (This rule will enable the players to anticipate 3's floor position and will help to simplify the regrouping.)

Diagram 175 illustrates Rule 3 governing our offensive regrouping.

4. The high-post position will be filled off the break by either 5 or 4. This is determined by the player, either 5 or 4, whose

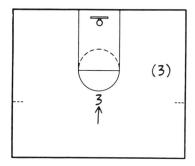

Diagram 174

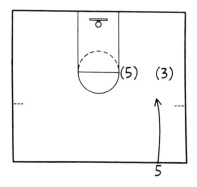

Diagram 175

break route is on the same side of the floor with 3 on the break setting up at the high-post position.

Diagram 176 illustrates Rule 4 governing our offensive regrouping.

5. Whenever the strong-side forward (3) fills the middle lane on the break and either 4 or 5 fills the outside lane to his right, they will interchange positions in regrouping.

Diagram 177 illustrates Rule 5 governing our offensive regrouping.

6. In the event 5 has established a high-post position, then 4 will automatically flow down to the baseline on the opposite side of the floor and establish a weak-side forward position. In

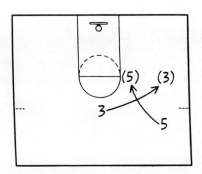

Diagram 176

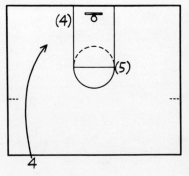

Diagram 177

the event 4 established a high-post position, then 5 will set up at the weak-side forward position.

Diagram 178 illustrates Rule 6 governing our offensive regrouping.

7. The guards' floor positions after a break are determined in the following manner: (a) the guard who goes deep on the break clears to the baseline and in regrouping fills the weak-side guard position; (b) the guard closest to the strong-side forward (3) sets up at the strong-side guard position.

Diagram 179 illustrates Rule 7a governing our offensive regrouping.

Diagram 180 illustrates Rule 7b governing our offensive regrouping.

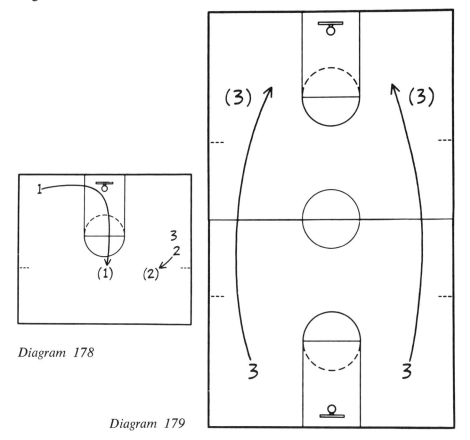

Diagram 178

Diagram 179

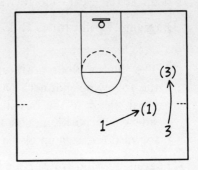

Diagram 180

OFFENSIVE TIPS TO PLAYERS

1. Take the "crip" or the short-range jump shot from the controlled break.
2. Never take the long-range jump shot off the controlled break.
3. The success of the controlled break depends upon getting the ball out fast. (Don't pass the ball to the corner.) Another very important factor in the break is *anticipation*—that is, when you think that your team is going to get the ball, move quickly to get the split second start on the defense.
4. Know that the longer and quicker the *outlet pass*, the more defensive men that are cut off.
5. Upon recovery of a loose ball, call "break" to alert others.
6. Get the ball to the middle.
7. Know that a pass is normally better than the dribble, though the dribble may be effective when past mid-court.
8. Players filling the outside lane go to the baseline and then come out.
9. Keep your passes up, chest high, and in front of the players to whom you are passing.

10. Whenever you are overplayed while looking for an outlet pass to start the break, clear out taking your men "deep."
11. Players filling the side lanes in the break stay *wide*.
12. Players filling the side lanes on the break, upon reaching the foul lane extended, cut to the basket on a diagonal cut.
13. Run under control; *do not draw a charging foul*.
14. Block out on the defensive board. All five players must do their job. Remember the break does not start until you get the ball.
15. The front lane cutters "stagger" their cuts, that is, they do not arrive at the scoring area at the same time. "Staggering" your cuts will double the chances of scoring.
16. Situations may develop due to defensive pressure, etc., but in general follow these patterns.

8

Coordinated Teaching
Drills for the
Flip-Flop Offense

The success of any offensive system is dependent upon the individual player and the execution of his offensive techniques. The daily practice sessions during the preseason and the season should contain breakdown drills of these techniques that will enable the players to become more proficient in their basic offensive maneuvers.

The late General Bob Neyland, University of Tennessee football coach and a great believer in fundamental drills, was once quoted as saying: "I have never used an offensive play in a game that has not been executed correctly in practice at least 500 times." This statement only tends to point out the emphasis that we, as coaches, must place upon the constant repetition of the basic fundamentals of the game in order to build a successful offensive system.

When we begin our preseason practice sessions and are going through our "installation" period (by this we mean breaking down the Flip-Flop Offense and teaching individual techniques and maneuvers) three fundamentals are emphasized: timing, finesse, and teamwork. These three fundamentals are the success of any offensive system and are developed only through constant repetition and the proper instruction.

In the diagrams that follow, we shall illustrate and discuss some of the coordinated teaching drills for the Flip-Flop Offense. Along with the illustrations and descriptions of the drills, we shall also discuss the individual offensive techniques that are so important to overall team execution.

GUARD-TO-GUARD DRILL

One of the most important and competitive drills of our Flip-Flop coordinated teaching drills is the guard-to-guard drill. The purpose of this drill is to teach correct faking, cutting and passing techniques in guard-to-guard movement.

The drill is set up with a line of guards filling both the strong-side guard (1) and the weak-side guard (2) positions. The first two guards in these respective lines step out and are the defensive players to start the drill and the next two men are the offensive players.

An offensive player is stationed at the high-post (5) position without a defensive man guarding him. This high-post man is stationary and is not eligible to receive a pass, shoot or dribble. His sole responsibility in this drill is that of a stationary screen for the offensive guards.

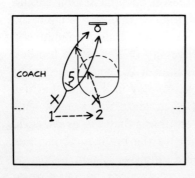

Diagram 181

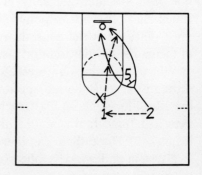

Diagram 182

Diagram 181 illustrates the floor positions for the guard-to-guard drill. The drill begins with offensive guard 1 passing to guard 2 and cutting off high-post man 5; 1 attempts to rub his defensive guard off high-post man 5, either with a cut down the lane or a back-side cut. In the event that guard 1 is successful in rubbing his defensive guard off on high-post man 5, then guard 2 passes over his defensive guard to guard 1 under the basket for the lay-up. The ability of guard 2 to pass to an open man while under pressure from a defensive guard is of paramount importance to any team and should be practiced daily.

The coach should station himself at an angle between the guard and the high-post man so as to determine whether or not the guard has executed the proper techniques in rubbing his man off on the high-post man.

The drill continues with the defensive guards going to the back of the guard line where they will become offensive guards the next time they come to the front of the line. Offensive guards 1 and 2 fill the defensive guard slots and the following two guards in the lines become the offensive guards. The drill continues on the same side of the floor until each player in the strong-side guard line has played both as an offensive and a defensive player. After this the high-post man 5 moves across the lane and the drill continues from the opposite side of the floor with the passing guard becoming the cutting guard (Diagram 182).

The coach can add to the effectiveness of this drill by grading and scoring the offensive and defensive guards. The offensive guard is awarded one point each time he rubs his defensive guard off on the high-post man. The defensive guard is awarded one point each time the offensive guard fails to rub him off on the high-post man. The offensive guard in the weak-side guard line is awarded one point each time he makes a perfect pass over his defensive guard to the cutting guard. The defensive guard in the weak-side guard line is awarded one point each time he intercepts or deflects any pass made from a guard to a guard. A manager may be stationed under the goal with a score card to record the points awarded to the players by the coach. The first player to reach a score of 10 points during this drill wins the scoring game and the coach can reward him during the practice session.

NOTE: The following are some of the important executive techniques that should be taught during this drill:

The guard-to-guard pass to start the drill should always be made to the receiving guard chest high and outside. The weak-side guard before receiving the pass should move his defensive guard inward toward the basket a couple of steps before coming back for the pass. The weak-side guard after receiving the pass from the cutting guard should put the ball over his head for a possible return pass to the cutting guard.

The strong-side guard, who is known as the cutting guard in this drill, looks for a return pass on his cut off the high-post man with his arm extended high as a target.

THE GUARD HIGH-POST CUT DRILL

The guard high-post cut is an excellent three-on-three drill involving an offensive guard, a forward, and a high-post man with defensive men guarding them. Diagram 183 illustrates our guard high-post cut drill. 1 sets up at a strong-side guard position, 3 sets up at a strong-side forward position, and 5 sets up at the high-post position.

Guard 1 starts this drill with a pass to forward 3 and a cut to the basket attempting to rub his defensive man off on the high-post man. 3 after receiving 1's pass faces the basket and prepares to feed 1 on his cut to the basket. Guard 1 can take either the inside or back side cutting route off high-post man 5, depending upon the position of his defensive guard. Emphasis during this drill should be placed upon guard 1's faking and footwork without the ball after his pass to the forward.

NOTE: It is important that guard 1, after making his pass to the forward, take two or three "stutter" steps away from the forward into his defensive guard. This maneuver enables guard 1 to line his defensive guard up with the high-post man and makes for an effective "rub-off" maneuver.

Guard 1 on his cut off the high post should brush against high-post 5's elbow to insure a positive brush-off of his defensive guard.

Guard 1, after he has executed his "rub-off" on the high-post man, should look directly at the forward on his cut to the basket with his inside arm extended high for a passing target.

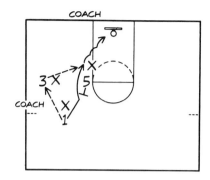

Diagram 183   *Diagram 184*

Two coaches are needed to supervise this drill effectively. One of the coaches should be stationed outside at mid-court to instruct guard 1 on his "rub-off" techniques with high-post man 5. The other coach should be stationed underneath the basket in order to instruct guard 1 on the proper techniques in cutting to the basket and receiving the ball (Diagram 184).

FORWARD HIGH-POST DRILL

The forward high-post drill helps to coordinate the offensive movement between the strong-side forward 3 and the high-post man 5. These two players work together as a unit against two defensive players. The coach starts the drill by passing to forward 3, whose defensive man plays a passive defense until forward 3 receives the ball; he then plays as aggressively as possible; high-post man 5 holds his position until forward 3 receives the pass from the coach, high-post man 5 then steps across to screen for forward 3 and work a screen-and-roll two-on-two maneuver (Diagram 185, next page).

The drill continues until the offensive players have scored or the defensive players have gained possession of the ball. The players then move to the opposite side of the floor where the coach starts the drill again with a pass to the forward.

After this drill has been run from both sides of the floor, the players exchange positions, the offensive players becoming defensive players, and the defensive players becoming the offensive players. Competition can be added to this drill by setting eight field goals as a game limit and penalizing the losing team with laps around the playing floor. A coach's imagination can furnish many gimmicks that will make this drill more interesting and competitive.

TANDEM POST DRILLS

The hub of the Flip-Flop Offense is the high and low post, the high-post and the weak-side forward positions whose offensive floor positions form a tandem post alignment. The timing and teamwork between these players is important to the success of the Flip-Flop Offense.

Diagram 186 illustrates the first of our tandem post drills. The coach or manager acts as the feeder and assumes a guard position. We position our pivot men at the high-post and the low-post positions with defensive men guarding them. The coach starts the drill by passing the ball to the high-post man, who turns and faces up to the basket. He can either feed low-post man 4 coming across the lane or drive to the basket. This is an excellent two-on-two drill for our pivot men and helps them to coordinate their offensive post movement.

NOTE: It should be emphasized to the high-post man that he should turn and face up and make his offensive move as quickly as possible.

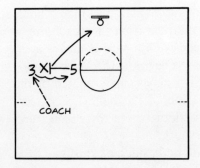

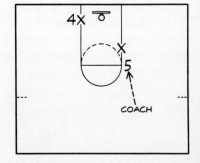

Diagram 185   *Diagram 186*

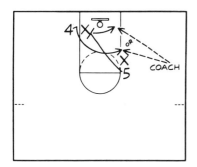

Diagram 187

The high-post man should be instructed to feed low-post man 5 whenever possible in the middle of the lane. When he receives the ball in the middle of the lane, he will be able to go either left or right with his offensive move.

Diagram 187 illustrates the second tandem post drill, the post exchange drill. We again set up our pivot men at the high- and low-post positions with defensive players guarding them. The coach in this drill stations himself at a forward position and the pass into the pivot is made from a forward position. The coach will key the post maneuver by slapping the ball. Upon hearing the coach slap the ball, high-post man 5 rolls down and screens low-post man 4's defensive man; low-post 4 comes over the top of the screen looking for a pass from the coach and a short jump shot, while high-post 5 rolls underneath the basket after setting his screen on low-post 4's defensive man.

NOTE: Low-post man 4 should be instructed to line his defensive man up for high-post 5's screen with a baseline foot fake to the basket. If high-post 5 or low-post 4 is not open after the post exchange, then the coach can pass to the high-post man and let him operate one on one.

WEAK-SIDE DRILL

This is an excellent offensive drill that can be utilized either with or without defensive players. In preseason practice sessions, we use this drill as a "dummy" drill; that is, without defensive players. After our guards and forwards have acquired their techniques and timing through the "dummy" practice drills, we apply the defense. In illustrating and discussing the weak-side drill, we shall discuss our "dummy" weak-side drill and how we utilize it in our pre-season practice sessions.

The weak-side drill that we run daily during our preseason practice sessions is divided into three phases. The first phase of the weak-side drill is illustrated in Diagram 188.

An offensive guard (2) is set up at the weak-side guard position, and an offensive forward (3) is set up at the weak-side forward position. Since we work almost entirely in the preseason on our offensive techniques and timing, the guard and forward have no defensive men guarding them.

The first phase of the weak-side drill starts with forward (3) breaking out, looking for a pass from guard (2). The guard passes the ball to the forward and cuts sharply to the basket looking for a return pass and a lay-up. If the pass is made, the forward rebounds the ball after the guard's lay-up, and the forward and guard go to the end of their respective lines.

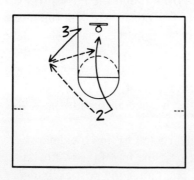

Diagram 188

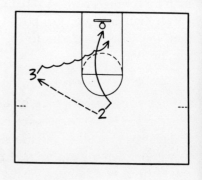

Diagram 189

NOTE: Some important offensive techniques we teach in the weak-side drill are: the forward, in moving out to meet the ball, should have his outside hand extended as a target for the guard to look for in passing to him. The forward, in passing to the guard who is cutting to the basket, should always pass the ball to him chest high and head him.

The guard, in passing the ball to the forward, should always aim at the forward's outside hand he has extended as a target. The guard should use only a short follow-through with his pass to the forward. An exaggerated follow-through only tends to decrease the guard's quickness and to delay his cut to the basket. The guard, after making his pass to the forward, should take a step away from the direction of his pass in an attempt to open up his cutting route to the basket. The guard, after taking the step in the opposite direction of the pass, should then move off that leg in executing his cut to the basket. The guard will shoot the ball with either hand, depending upon the side of the floor from which he receives the ball.

Diagram 189 illustrates the second phase of the weak-side drill.

Guard (2) passes the ball to forward (3) and executes his cut to the basket. Forward (3), after receiving the ball, faces up to the basket, squaring both his head and shoulders with the basket. Forward (3) executes a quick fake toward the baseline with his head, shoulders, and baseline foot. He then drives across the lane for either a lay-up or a jump shot. Guard (2) serves as the rebounder after the forward shoots the ball. Guard (2) and forward (3) both go to the end of their respective lines at the conclusion of this maneuver.

NOTE: It is important that the forward execute the proper faking techniques before his drive across the middle of the lane. After the forward executes a head and shoulder fake, he should use a short jab-step fake with his baseline foot. The forward's pivot foot should remain stationary while he is executing his jab-step fake. The coach should observe the forward's pivot foot very closely during this drill and call all traveling violations to his attention. The jab-step fake is an excellent offensive maneuver, but many players find it difficult to use without dragging or sliding the pivot foot.

Diagram 190 illustrates the third phase of the weak-side drill.

This drill starts in the same manner as the first two phases, with a pass from the guard to the forward and a cut to the basket.

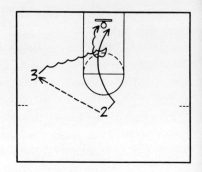

Diagram 190

Forward (3) faces the basket and executes the same fakes and dribble across the lane as he executes in phase two of the weak-side drill. In this particular drill, we also teach our forwards the "dribble reverse" maneuver. This is an excellent maneuver for the forward whenever the defensive man has cut off his drive across the middle of the lane. In executing the "dribble reverse" maneuver, the forward starts his drive across the lane, stops and pivots quickly while changing his dribble to his opposite hand, reverses in the opposite direction, and lays the ball up. Guard (2) serves as the rebounder after forward (3) shoots; they both then go to the end of their respective lines.

An important point to teach the forwards on the "dribble reverse" maneuver is to attain quickness on the change-over from the dribble. The change-over dribble should be executed with the ball kept as low to the floor as possible. We instruct our forwards to execute a half-body turn after their stop before changing the ball over to the opposite hand on their reverse. This half-body turn technique helps to speed up the "dribble reverse" and to add needed quickness to the maneuver.

BIG MAN–LITTLE MAN DRILL

Many basketball teams fail to take advantage of the mismatch situations that develop during the course of a basketball game. These situations occur when there is a defensive switch, and a little defensive guard switches off and has to guard either a tall offensive forward or post man. The guard-to-the-corner option of the Flip-Flop Offense is designed to set up these mismatch situations. The big man–little man drill is an excellent teaching drill to instruct the guards, forwards, and centers in the techniques for taking advantage of the mismatch situations.

The drill starts with an offensive guard (G^1) setting up on the baseline with a defensive guard guarding him and a forward or center (4) setting up at the high post with a defensive player guarding him. The coach who is stationed at a high forward position is the feeder in this drill. He passes to G^1 to start the drill.

NOTE: The coach from this high forward position has excellent floor coverage from which to observe both G^1 and the offensive high-post man in their offensive techniques (Diagram 191).

G^1, before receiving a pass from the coach, should always take his defensive man in two steps toward the basket and then come back to receive the pass from the coach. High-post man 4, upon seeing G^1 receive the pass on the baseline, comes across quickly to set a screen on G^1's defensive guard. G^1 comes over the top of 4's screen looking for a defensive switch and a mismatch. In the event there is a defensive switch, high-post man 4 will roll to the basket with the little defensive guard on his back. G^1 will then feed high-post man 4 a high lob pass on his roll to the basket. The drill continues until the offensive players score or the defensive players gain possession of the ball. After this the defensive guard and high-post

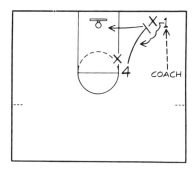

Diagram 191

man move to the baseline to await their turn to become offensive players. The offensive guard and high-post man become defensive players.

NOTE: To add to the effectiveness of this drill the coach can signal to the defensive men whether or not to switch. Hand signals such as raising one finger to indicate a switch and two fingers for the defensive men to slide through and not to switch can be utilized. In the event the defensive men do not switch, G^1 looks for the short jump shot or drive to the basket. The hand signals by the coach to the defensive players help to keep the offensive players off balance and help to stimulate actual changing game type of defensive play.

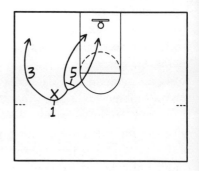

Diagram 192

CAT AND MOUSE DRILL

The cat and mouse drill is our most effective drill in teaching our offensive guards to maneuver without the ball. In this particular drill, which includes the strong-side guard, the strong-side forward, and the high-post man, guard 1 is the only offensive player with a defensive man on him. Guard 1 starts the drill with a pass to forward 3 and may then take one of three cutting routes: the inside of the high-post man, the back-side of the high-post man, or the outside of the forward. These cutting routes are illustrated in Diagram 192.

Guard 1 must rub his defensive man off on either the high-post man (5) or the forward (3). Guard 1 has a distinct advantage over his defensive guard because the defensive guard does not know which of the three cutting routes guard 1 will take on his cut. Whenever guard 1 rubs his defensive guard off, then forward 3 feeds him the ball for a lay-up.

In the event guard 1 fails to rub his defensive guard off on his cutting route, we penalize guard 1 with a lap around the playing floor. This extra incentive for our defensive guard has added the competition to the drill that tends to make for aggressive defensive and offensive play.

NOTE: After guard 1 has rubbed his defensive man off, the drill starts over with new personnel at the strong-side forward, high post and strong-side guard. Guard 1, after completing his rub-off maneuver, comes back outside and takes the defensive guard's position. The defensive guard then goes to the end of the offensive guard (1) line.

Two coaches, one underneath the goal and the other outside, should closely supervise guard 1 on his movements without the ball.

BIG CIRCLE DRILL

This pressure drill is one of our most aggressive and competitive drills. The big circle drill enables us to utilize not only our guards but also our centers and forwards in pressure situations.

The drill starts with an offensive player and a defensive player in each of the three circles on the basketball court. The circles are located at each end of the gymnasium at the free-throw line and one at the mid-court area (Diagram 193).

The offensive players in the circles have a basketball which they attempt to dribble (with good body control) around the inside of their respective circles. The defensive men inside each circle attempt to either steal or deflect the ball away from the dribbler. The defensive men are encouraged to use their hands and bodies and are allowed to make good body contact with the offensive men. Again it should be emphasized to the offensive men or dribblers that they must stay inside the circles and maintain possession of the basketball.

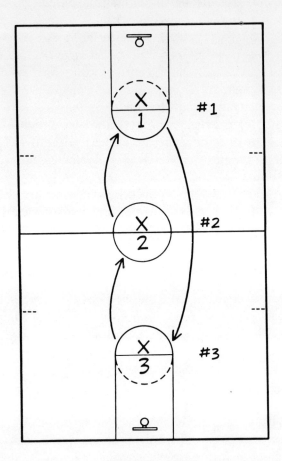

Diagram 193

The big circle drill stimulates the pressure type of game conditions and will help the offensive players to adjust to rough body contact while maintaining possession of the basketball. Many times during the course of a season, a team will encounter rough, aggressive defensive play in control type situations. A team will have difficulty adjusting and offensing this aggressive type of defensive play unless they are exposed to it during their daily practice sessions.

NOTE: A scoring system is also utilized during this drill as an incentive for both the offensive and defensive men. The offensive men or dribblers are awarded one point each if they maintain possession of the basketball for 30 seconds. The defensive men are awarded one point each if they are successful in either stealing or deflecting the ball, or forcing the dribbler outside of the circle boundaries.

A manager is stationed at half-court with a stop watch and a whistle. He clocks all three circles simultaneously and at the conclusion of the timed 30 seconds, the manager blows the whistle and awards the points.

The rotation of the drill is as follows: the circles are numbered 1, 2, and 3. Number 1 dribbler goes to circle 3 to play defense, and number 1 defensive player remains in circle 1 as the dribbler. Number 2 dribbler moves to circle 1 as the defensive player and circle 2 defensive player remains in circle 1 as the dribbler. Number 2 dribbler moves to circle 1 as the defensive player, and circle 2 defensive player remains in circle 2 as the dribbler. Number 3 dribbler goes to circle 2 as the defensive player, and the circle 2 defensive player remains in circle 2 as the dribbler.

GUARD PRESSURE DRILLS

"Body-Checking" Drill

The "body-checking" drill is a guard pressure type of drill that helps acclimate our guards to such game type conditions as body-checking, bumping, hands on body, etc. These simulated game conditions help prepare our guards to adjust to body contact during their cutting routes to the basket.

The drill begins with two lines of guards lined up two steps behind the half-court line. The coach should set up at a high forward position on one side of the floor, and a manager can set up at a high forward position on the other side of the floor. The coach and the managers do not have defensive men guarding them as they are receivers for the guards to pass to before cutting to the basket (Diagram 194).

The first two players in the guard lines step out and set up as "body-checkers" at the half-court line. The next two guards are offensive guards who attempt to advance the ball into the front court and pass the ball to either the coach or the manager. The offensive guards will make their pass and cut to the basket looking for a return pass on a give-and-go maneuver. The two "body-checkers" will use whatever body contact necessary to deter or slow down the offensive guards on their cutting routes to the basket.

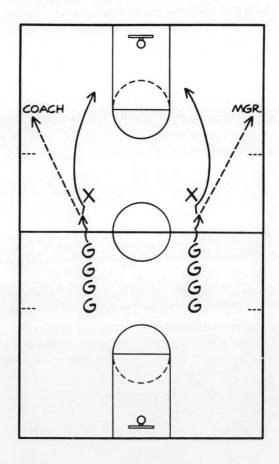

Diagram 194

NOTE: The offensive guards should be taught to pass and then slide away from pressure on their cut to the basket. They should be instructed never to fight the "body-check" by a defensive man which only tends to bog down an offense and cause congestion in the scoring area.

The rotation for the "body-checking" drill is the same as many of our other half-court drills. The "body-checkers" go to the back of the guard line and the offensive guards in turn become the "body-checkers."

Outside Shoulder Drill

Many modern coaches subscribe to the theory of placing their defensive guards on the outside shoulder of the offensive guard with the ball. This is an excellent method of defensing the guard-to-forward pass. We try to simulate this defensive situation in one of our guard pressure drills. We call this drill the outside shoulder drill, and it is an excellent four-on-four drill.

Diagram 195 illustrates our outside shoulder drill, a four-on-four drill with two offensive guards and two offensive forwards with defensive men guarding them. The offensive forwards (3 and 4) are both set up at the strong-side forward position with the defensive forwards overplaying them. The drill is started with guard 1 having the ball and his defensive guard on his outside shoulder.

He passes the ball to guard 2 and executes a "hook-back" maneuver to open up the congested area for guard 2 to come on a quick dribble before his defensive guard can slide over on his outside shoulder and prevent his pass to forward 3. In the event that guard 2 cannot feed forward 3, then he makes a quick pass back to guard 1 who passes to forward 4 on the opposite side of the floor. After guard 1 or 2 has made a successful pass to either forward 3 or 4, he then cuts to the basket on a give-and-go maneuver. If the guard is not open, then the ball comes back out front and the drill starts over again with new offensive personnel filling the offensive guard and forward positions.

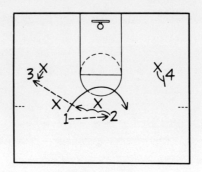

Diagram 195

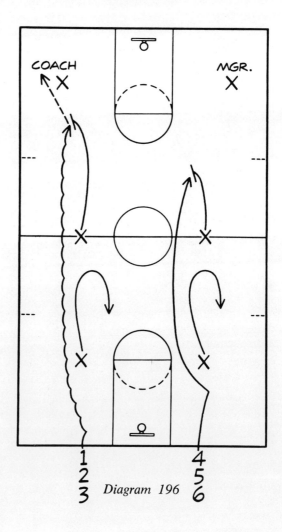

Diagram 196

Guard-Obstacle Course Drill

This is a guard pressure drill we refer to as our guard-obstacle course drill. We rely on this drill a lot during the course of a season in our practice sessions to help our guards react against extreme pressure. This drill is an excellent full-court pressure drill that can also serve as an excellent conditioner.

The drill starts with a line of offensive guards underneath the basket. Two defensive guards are stationed on each side of the free-throw line extended. Two defensive guards are stationed at the mid-court line. Two coaches or a coach and a manager are stationed at the far end of the playing floor at high forward positions and even with the free-throw line extended with two "passive" defensive players guarding them (Diagram 196).

The first two guards in the line underneath the basket step out and are offensive guards. They attempt to advance the ball up the court against a stacked pressure defense and pass to either the coach or the manager. The first two defensive players stationed at the free-throw line extended pick the two offensive guards up tight and pressure them. These front-line defense men are free to gamble for possible steals and they may double-team either offensive guard if they so desire. The defensive area these two front-line guards are responsible for is from the free-throw line extended to two steps this side of the mid-court line. After the two front-line defensive players who are pressuring the two offensive guards reach the area two steps this side of the mid-court area, the two defensive players drop off and are out of the play. The two offensive guards continue up court and the two defensive players at mid-court pick them up tight and pressure them. These two defensive players attempt to prevent the two offensive guards from passing to either the coach or manager. The two defensive players guarding the coach and the manager play only a "passive" defense and do not closely contest a pass to the coach or the manager. The offensive guards must penetrate the head of the key area before making their pass.

A scoring system is also kept during this drill as an incentive to both the offense and the defense. If the offensive guards are successful in advancing the ball up the court and making their pass, each offensive guard is awarded one point. Each defensive player is awarded one point for a steal, and the defensive player automatically exchanges positions with the offensive guard from whom he stole the ball during the play. The defensive player becomes the offensive guard and the offensive guard who lost the ball takes the defensive player's position on the floor. In the event two defensive guards steal the ball in a double-team situation, then each of the defensive players are awarded one-half point and they both go to offense. This drill is a timed drill, and the player with the most points when the manager blows the whistle signaling the time limit wins the drill.

The rotation of the guard obstacle course drill is as follows: The two offensive guards who advanced the ball become the "passive" defensive players guarding the coach and the manager. The two passive defensive players move to the mid-court area and assume the position of mid-court defenders. The two mid-court defensive players move into the back-court and fill the two defensive positions at the free-throw line extended. The first two defenders, who dropped off at the mid-court area and who were initially lined up at the free-throw line, go to the end of the offensive line underneath the basket during the rotation.

The time limit for this drill may vary, depending upon practice time allotment, team experience, and the enthusiasm and hustle of players during the drill.

FORWARD PRESSURE DRILLS

"Challenge" Drill

One of the most devastating defensive weapons an offense will encounter during a season is a tight defensive overplay on an offensive forward. This defensive maneuver has succeeded in countering many of the modern offenses. The offensive forward can be almost completely inactivated by a strong overplay by a defensive forward.

The success our offense and our offensive forwards have experienced during the past seasons against this defensive overplay has been due mainly to the preparation they have received from the "challenge" drill. The "challenge" drill is our most effective forward pressure drill and a drill that teaches the offensive forward how to react against the tight defensive pressure overplay.

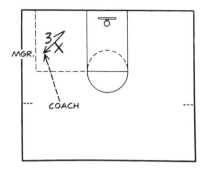

Diagram 197

The "challenge" drill is set up with an offensive forward stationed at the strong-side forward position with a defensive man pressuring and overplaying him. The coach is set up with the ball at the strong-side guard position with a good passing angle to the offensive forward. The coach does not have a defensive man guarding him in this drill and serves only as a feeder for the offensive forward. A manager is stationed at the side of the court out of bounds with a stop watch and serves as the timer and scorekeeper for the drill (Diagram 197).

NOTE: You will notice the perforated line markings in Diagram 197. These lines are drawn on the court by the coach before starting the drill with either chalk or tape. They serve as boundary lines for the offensive forward during this drill as he is not allowed to step either on or outside these boundary lines.

The drill begins with the offensive forward (3) setting up at a floor position lower than the strong-side forward position with the defensive forward tightly overplaying him. The offensive forward's responsibility in this drill is to free himself from the defensive forward and receive a pass from the coach inside the closed boundary area. The defensive forward's responsibility is to prevent the offensive forward from receiving a pass for a timed five-second period or to force the offensive forward to the outside of the boundary area to receive a pass from the coach.

The manager stationed on the side of the court times each group and awards the points to either the offensive or the defensive forward. If the offensive forward is successful in freeing himself, he is awarded one point, and if the defensive forward is successful in his overplay, he is awarded one point. The offensive forward can be awarded two points in the event he executes a successful back-door break to the basket. The first player to be awarded eight points in the "challenge" drill is declared the winner. The drill can be started again if time is available.

The rotation of the drill is as follows: The offensive forward (3), if he is successful in freeing himself, remains as the offensive player and the defensive forward goes to the end of the defensive line. In the event the offensive forward (3) could not free himself, he then goes to the end of the defensive line, and the defensive forward who successfully defensed the offensive forward, moves to the offensive forward position.

Forward Possession Drill

The forward possession drill is a pressure drill in which the defensive forward allows the offensive forward to gain possession of the ball before applying the defensive pressure. This is an excellent one-on-one offensive drill for the forwards because it helps them to perfect their offensive moves with the ball against defensive pressure.

Diagram 198 illustrates the forward possession drill.

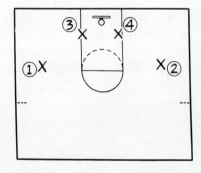

Diagram 198

The offensive floor stations are numbered one through four. These are the four floor areas where the forwards will work on their offensive maneuvers. The drill will begin at position 1 (strong-side forward) and will remain at this position until all of the forwards have played both offense and defense. The drill then moves to position 2 (strong-side forward), then to positions 3 and 4 (weak-side forward).

The rotation of the drill is as follows: The offensive forward remains on offense as long as he can score. The defensive forward goes to the rear of the defensive line, and a new defensive player steps out to pressure the offensive forward. In the event the offensive forward fails to score, he goes to the end of the defensive line and the defensive forward goes to the offensive line.

Many times in our practice sessions we have not had time to work with our forwards at all four of the floor areas. In these instances, we have worked with our forwards at one of the strong-side forward positions (1 or 3) and at one of the weak-side forward positions (3 or 4). These floor areas should be alternated during the season to allow the forwards to work from all four positions and from both sides of the floor.

POST PRESSURE DRILLS

Our post pressure drills help to prepare our pivot men for defensive post overplay and internal defensive pressure. They will encounter this pressure at one time or another during the course of a season. It is just as important that pivot men as well as guards be adept at maneuvering in pressure situations.

The first post pressure drill we will discuss is illustrated in Diagram 199 (next page).

The drill starts with five offensive players stationed in the five perimeter Flip-Flop floor positions. These five players remain stationary in their floor positions and can serve only as feeders in this particular drill. Offensive post man 4 sets up on the baseline with a defensive post man pressuring and body-checking him.

The defensive post man attempts to prevent the offensive post man from receiving a pass from any of the five perimeter feeders. The offensive post man's routes are also illustrated in the diagram,

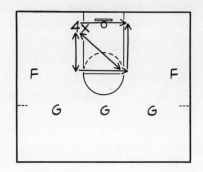

Diagram 199

and these are the routes the high-post man and the weak-side forward will run during the intiations of the Flip-Flop. The player stationed at the weak-side guard position and in the middle of the five perimeter feeders will start the drill with a pass either to his left or right, depending upon the initial route of the offensive pivot man. Whenever the offensive pivot man is successful in receiving a pass from a perimeter player, he passes the ball back to the perimeter player. After the successful pass into the pivot and the pass back outside, the offensive pivot man attempts to maneuver into position for another pass from one of the perimeter players. After the offensive pivot man has received five successful passes from the perimeter players, he is then replaced by a new offensive pivot man. This drill has enabled us to instruct our pivot men in two important fundamentals of offensive pivot play. The two fundamentals are that in receiving the ball, he should always move to meet each pass and should always put the ball over his head immediately after reception. In passing the ball the offensive pivot man should use an overhead pass whenever possible and he should not maintain possession too long inside on the pivot because of defensive sagging and floating.

"Power-Move" Drill

Diagram 200 illustrates another of our post pressure drills. We refer to this drill as our "power-move" drill.

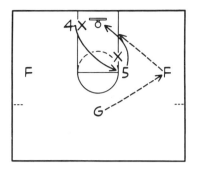

Diagram 200

The drill is set up with offensive player (5) at the high-post position and (4) at the weak-side forward position. Each of these two offensive players has a defensive man guarding him tightly and body-checking him. There are two perimeter players set up at the strong-side forward positions and one at the weak-side guard position at the head of the key. These perimeter players are stationary and can serve only as feeders for the two offensive post men.

The drill begins with the stationary guard at the top of the key passing to the stationary forward, after which high-post man 5 rolls down the lane. If he is open on his move down the lane, the forward feeds him a high lob pass, and he utilizes the power move.

The weak-side forward breaks up the middle of the lane to the high-post position, looking for a pass, and opens up the area underneath the basket for the high-post man. This maneuver is known as our "post rotation" option in our Flip-Flop man-to-man offense.

The "power-move" is an offensive maneuver that we teach our high-post men. In teaching the "power-move" we instruct the high-post man after rolling down the lane and receiving the pass from the forward to plant both feet on the floor, grasp the ball tightly with both hands, lean into his defensive man, and explode up to the basket. This maneuver will offer the high-post man many three point play opportunities. (In order that we may teach the "power-move" to our pivot men, it is important that they first develop strength in their arms, especially from the elbow down to the wrist and hands.) This strength coupled with an explosive jump will enable them simply to power the ball into the basket.

Index